STAINED

Copyright © 2024 by Colorful Paint.

All rights reserved. No part of this publication may be reproduced, distributed, or transmitted in any form or by any means, including photocopying, recording, or other electronic or mechanical methods, without the prior written permission of the publisher, except in the case of brief quotations embodied in critical reviews and certain other noncommercial uses permitted by copyright law.

WELCOME TO THE WORLD OF COLORFUL PAINT!

We have dedicated these first pages to enhance your experience with the book you have acquired. For us, it is crucial to provide you with all the information you need, so we ask you to take a few minutes and read carefully. We appreciate your attention!

PAPER QUALITY

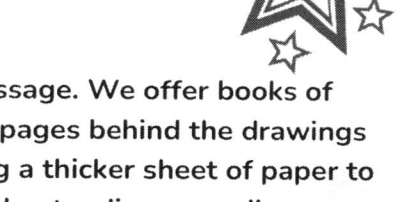

If you are using colored pencils, please disregard this message. We offer books of standard quality to provide affordable prices. Although the pages behind the drawings are black to prevent ink bleed-through, we recommend using a thicker sheet of paper to prevent marker or pen stains. We truly appreciate your understanding regarding our paper choice.

SHARE YOUR TALENT

At Colorful Paint, we love seeing how our drawings come to life as works of art. When you leave your comment, feel free to share photos so we can celebrate your creativity together. We're excited to see your artistic expression!

CONTACT US

If you have any questions or concerns, you can contact us at colorfulpaintpublishing@gmail.com We are here to assist you with anything you need.

@colorfulpaintpublishing

THANK YOU!

We really apreciatte for having purchased this book of "Stained Glass". Your support means a lot to us, feel free to share your thoughts and ratings.

SCAN ME / SCAN ME / SCAN ME / SCAN ME / SCAN ME / SCAN ME / SCAN ME / SCAN ME

RATE US HERE

NEWS, COLORING TIPS AND MORE

On our Instagram @colorfulpaintpublishing

Have fun with us on Instagram!

WAIT A MINUTE!

Before you start we recommend you use a thicker sheet of paper behind the page to prevent marker or pen bleed-through.

FREE DIGITAL COLORING BOOK +50 IMAGES

In gratitude for purchasing our book, we invite you to join our Facebook Community "Colorful Paint Publishing" to download the gift we have prepared for you.

Share your wonderful works of art with us!
Scan the QR code to join our Facebook Community or search us on Instagram and send a DM

  @colorfulpaintpublishing

SCAN ME

This Coloring Book belongs to:

_____

_____

COLOR TEST PAGE

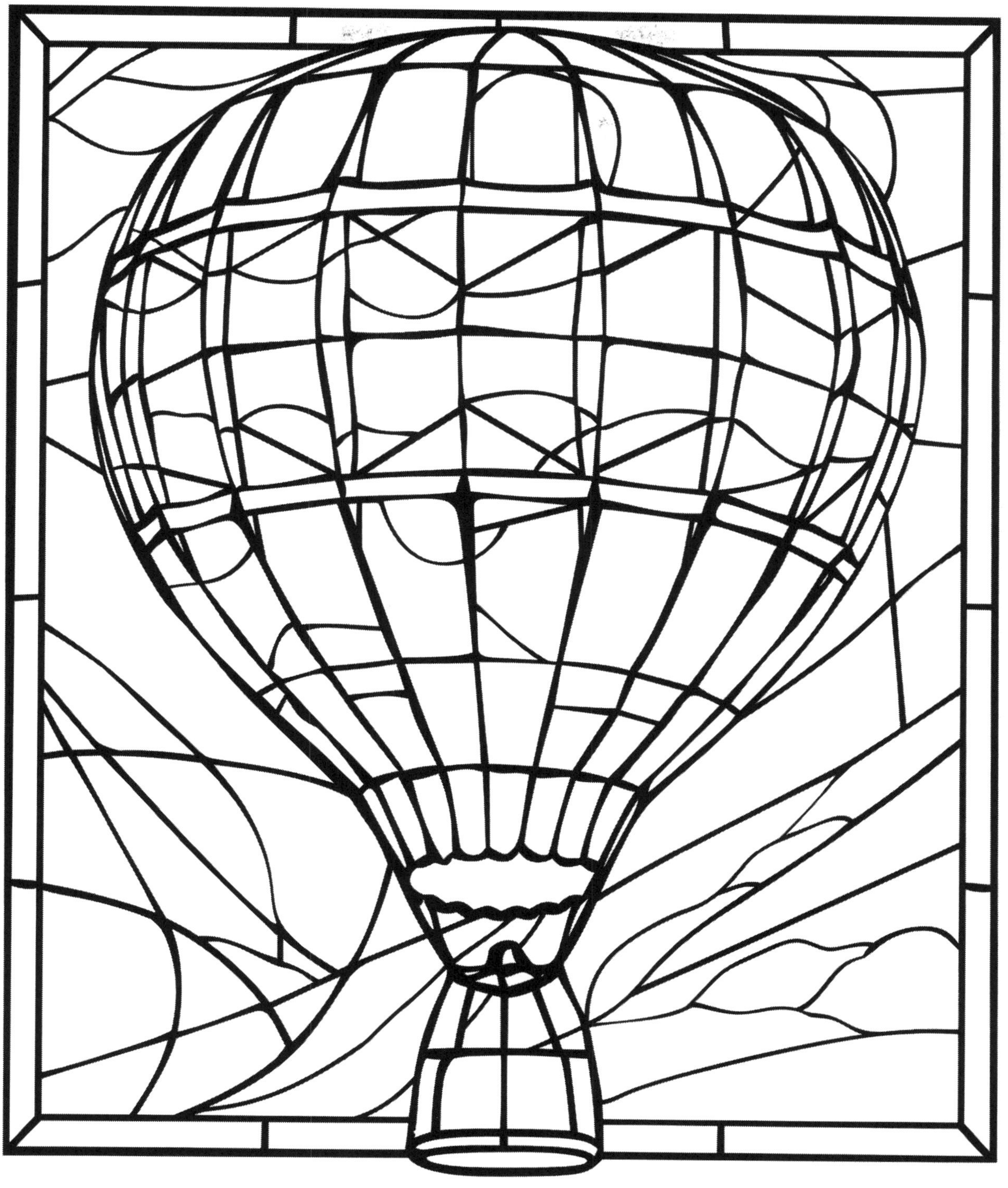

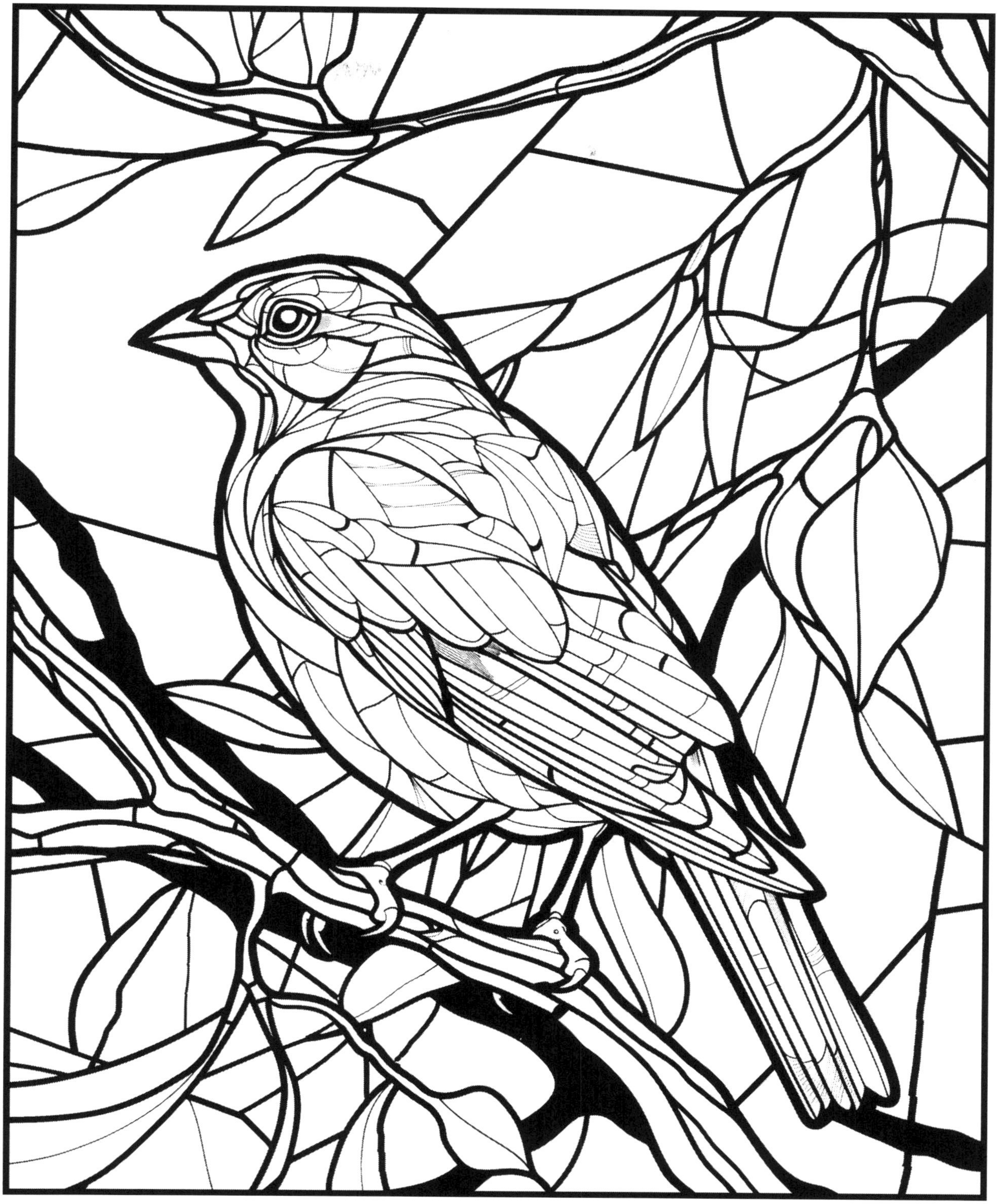

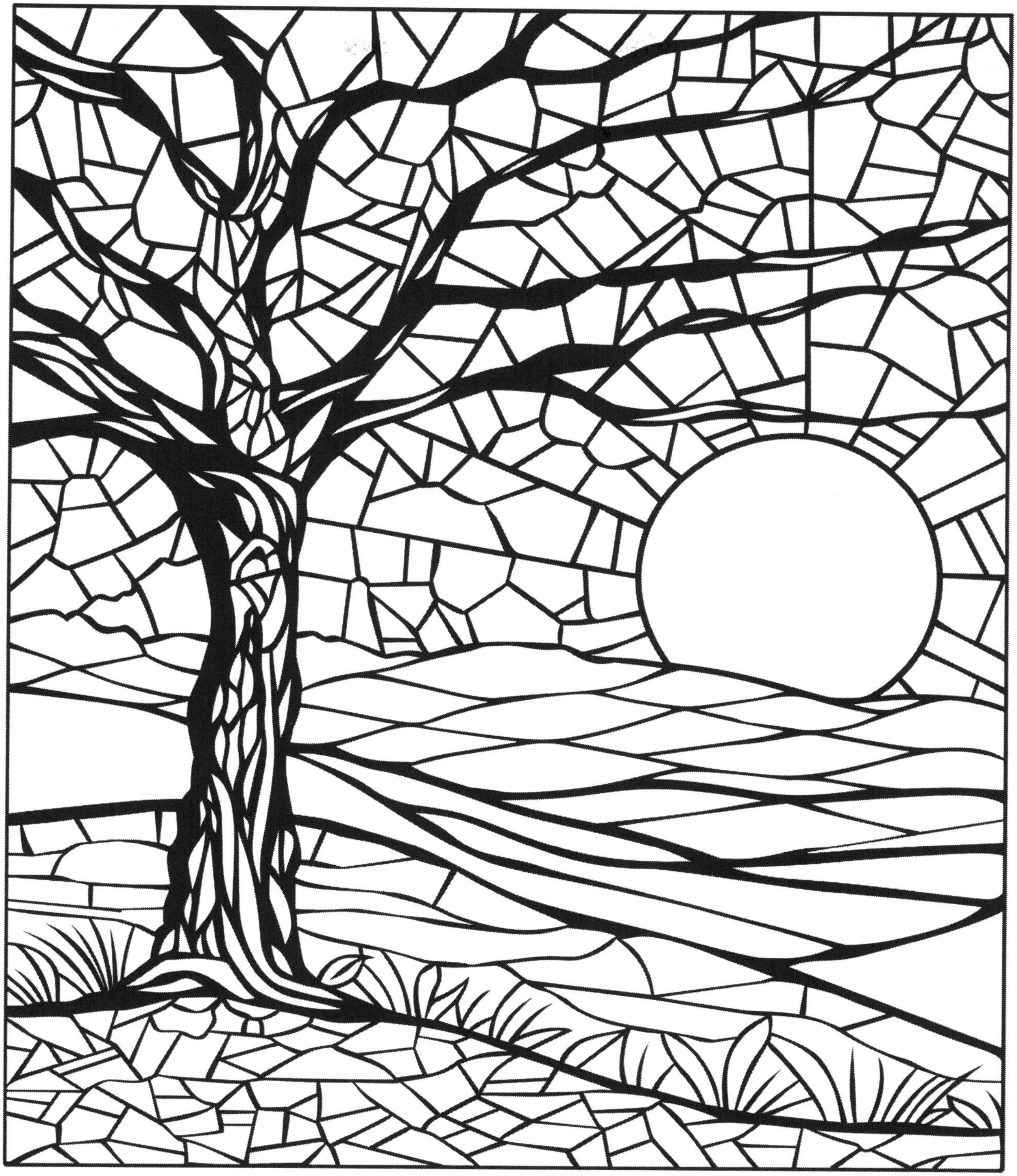

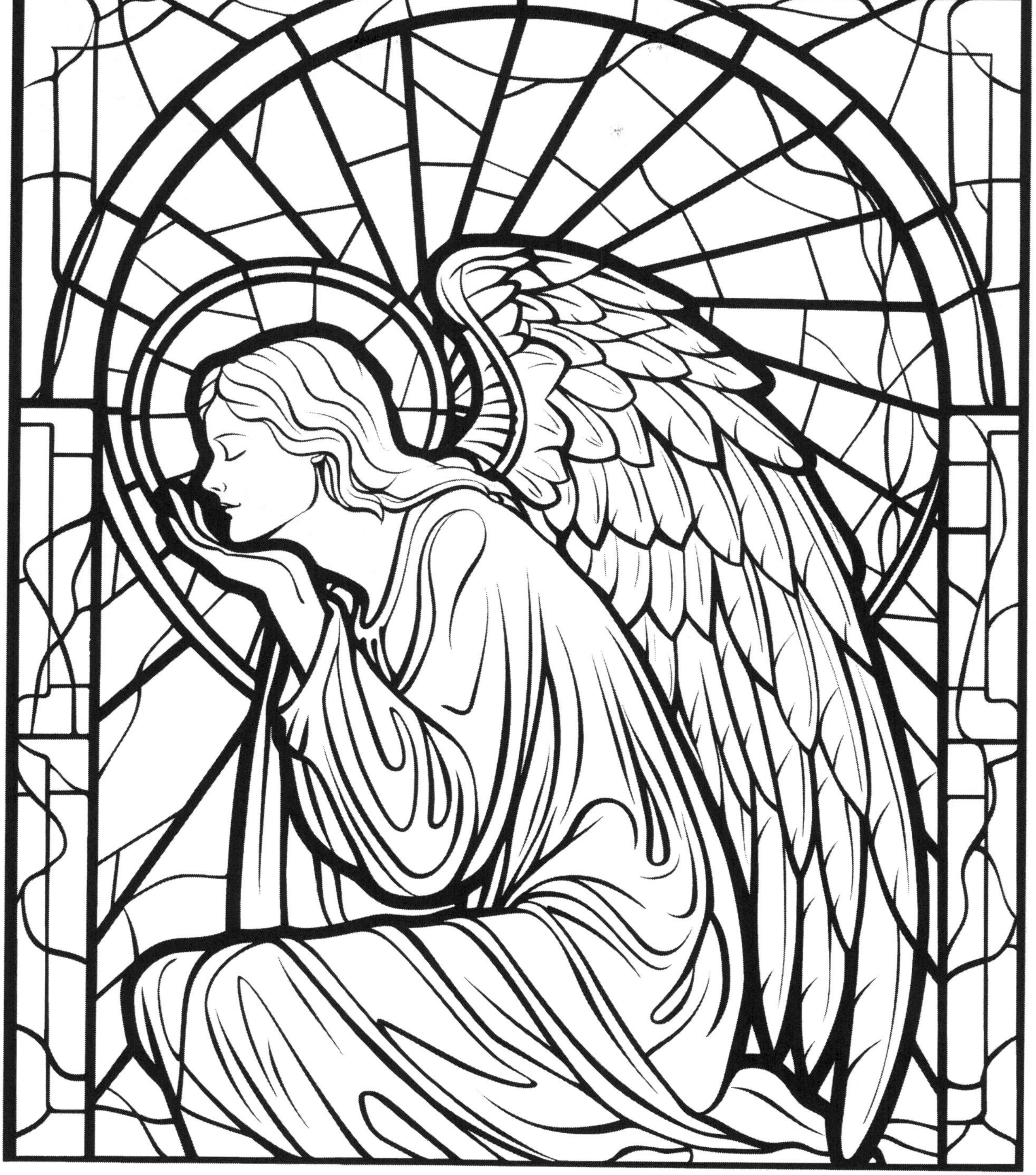

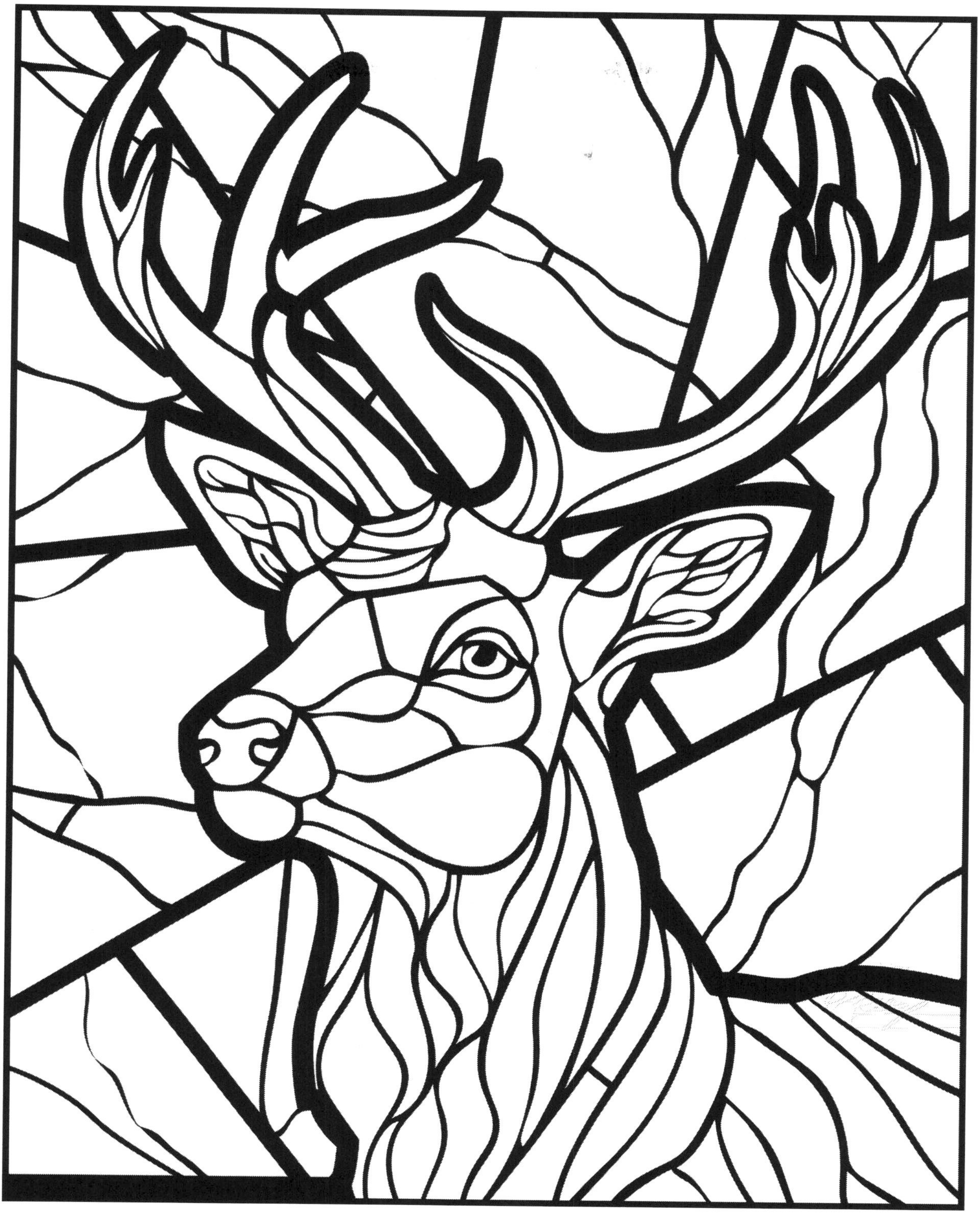

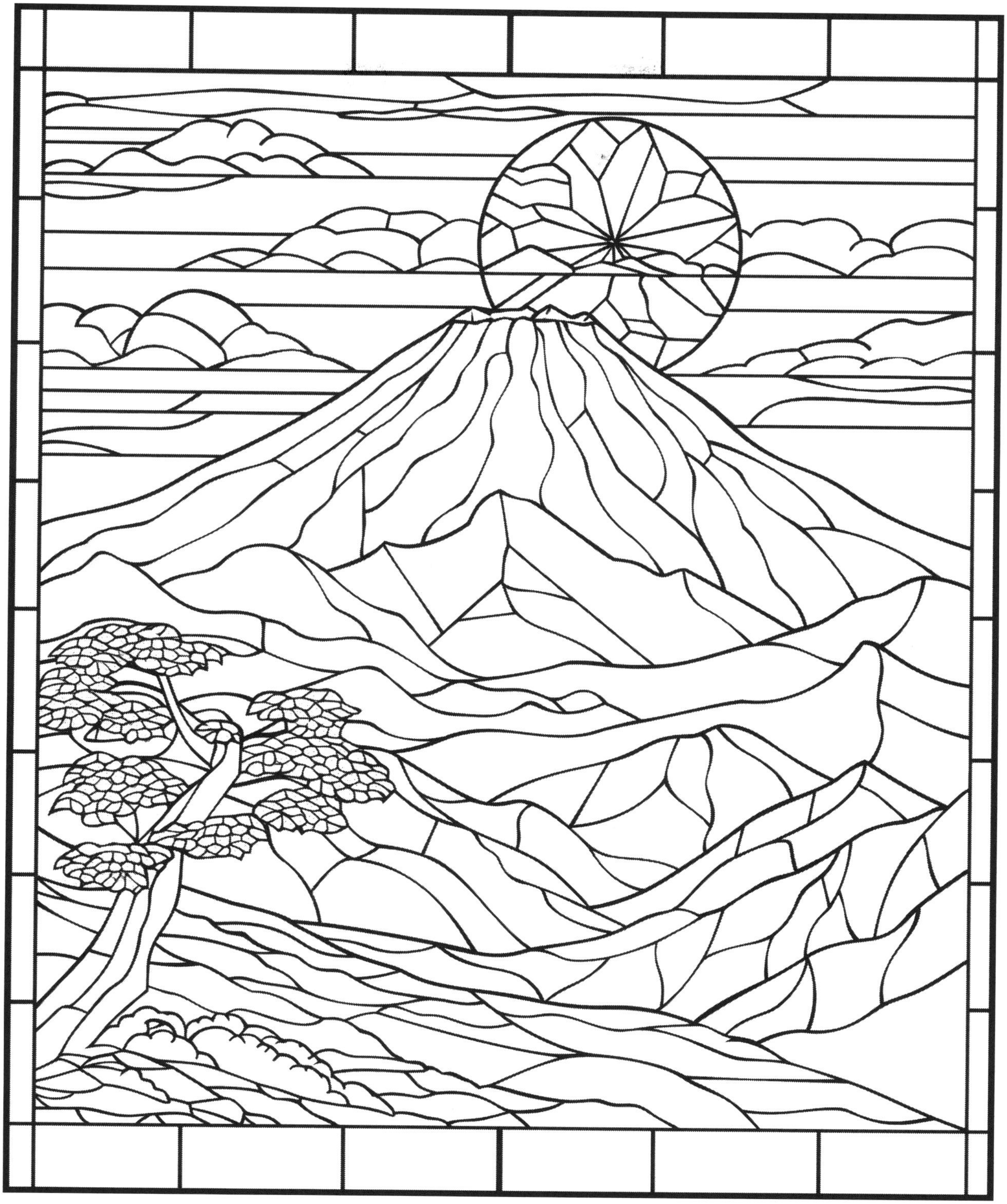

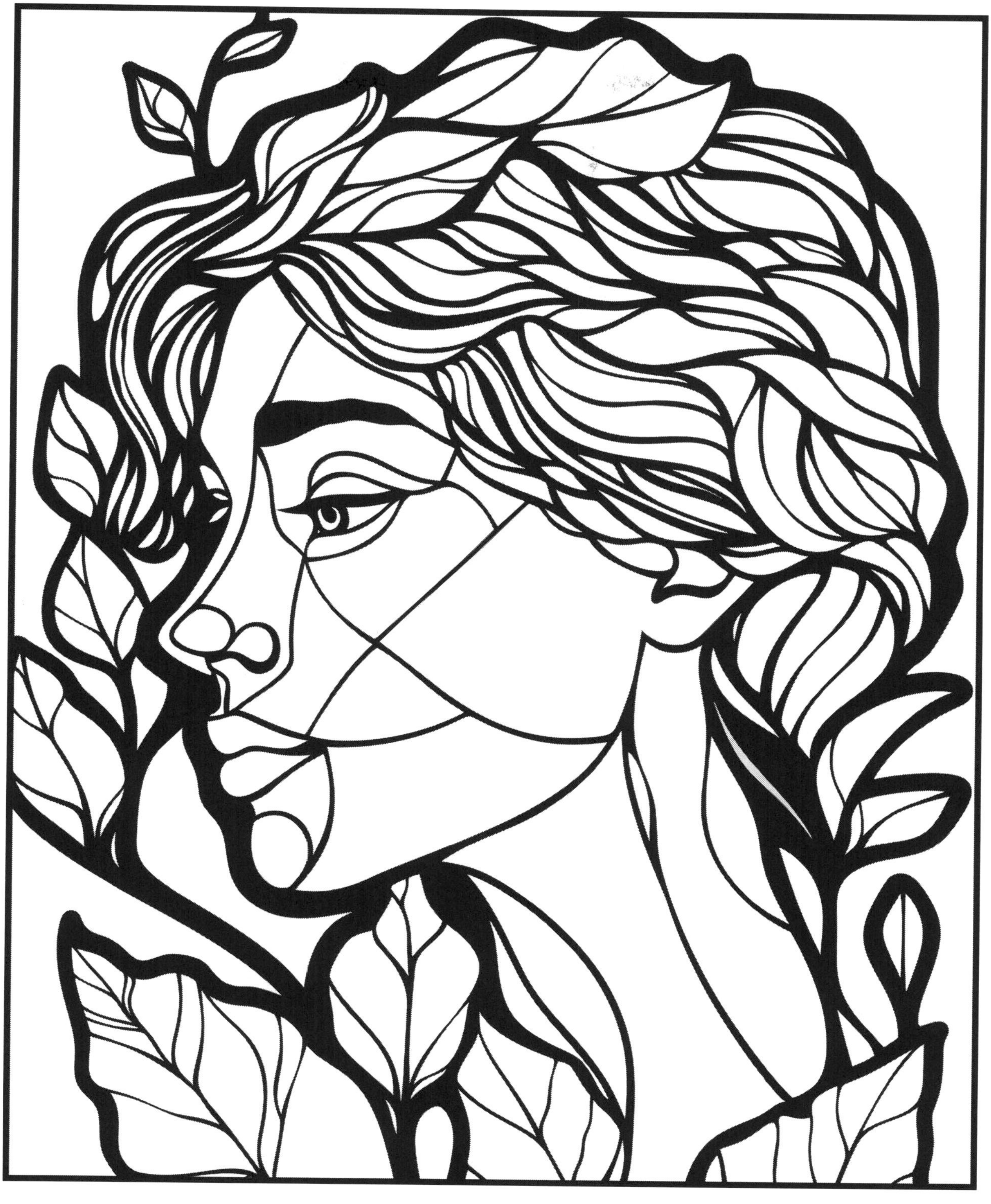

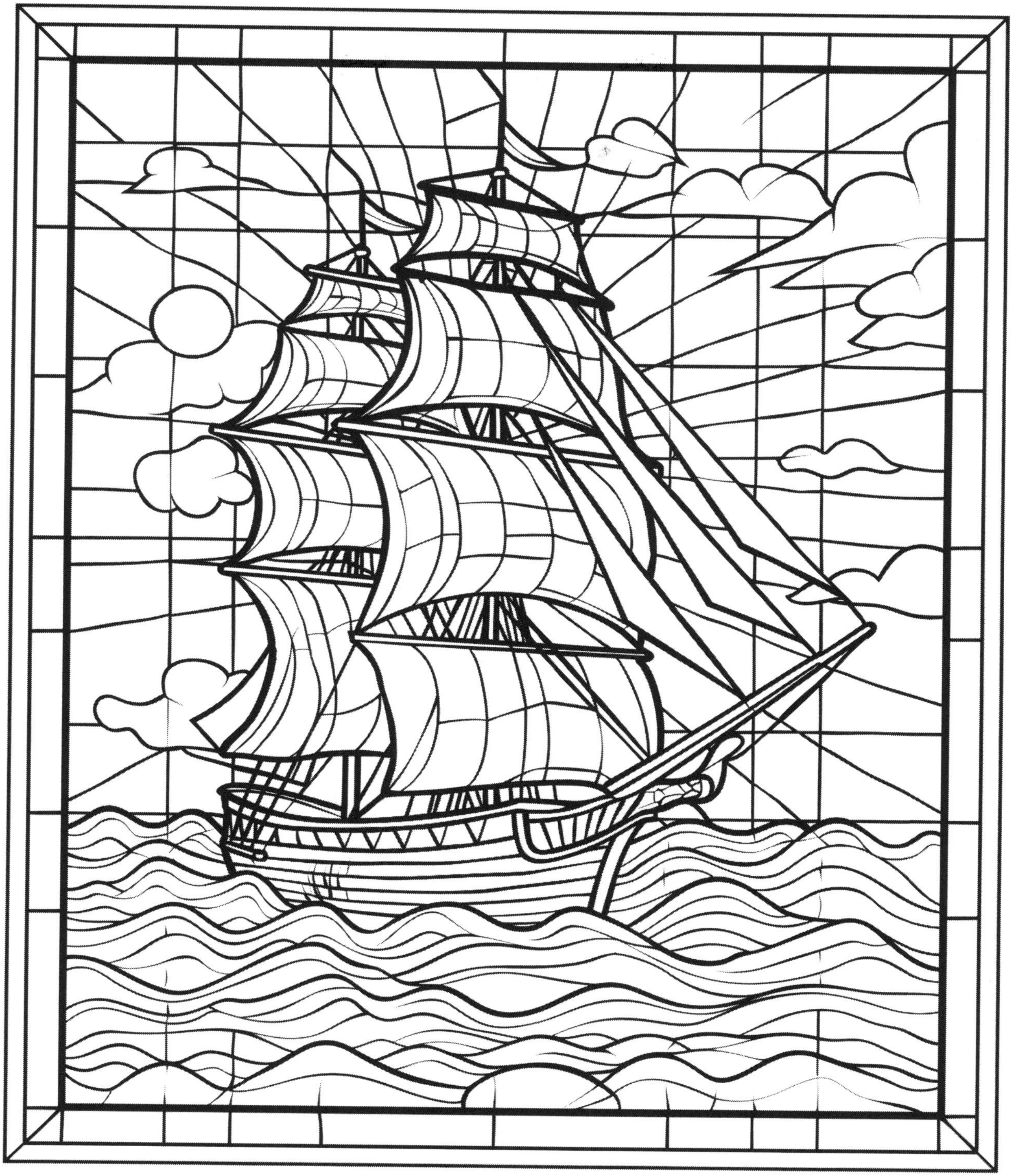

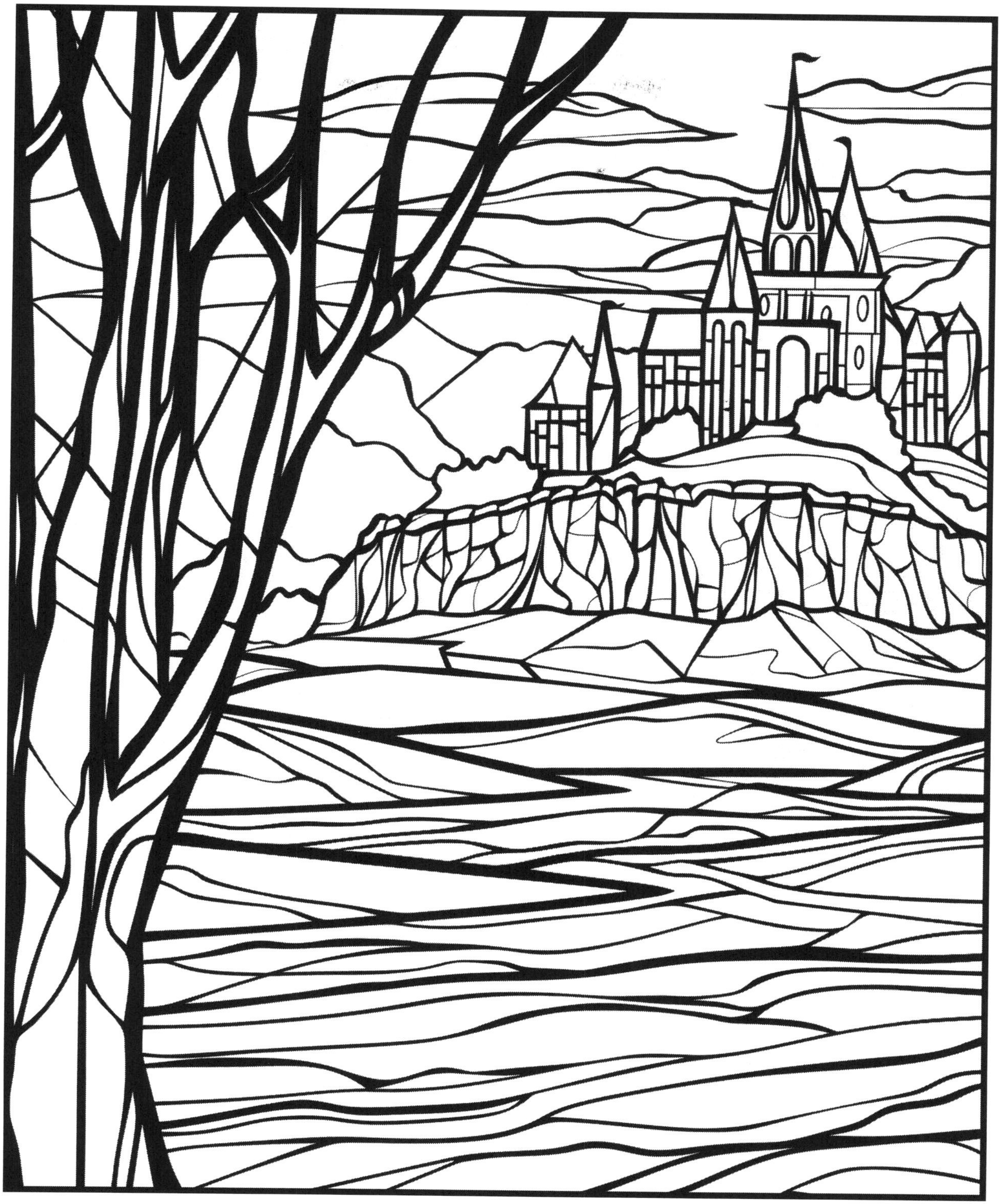

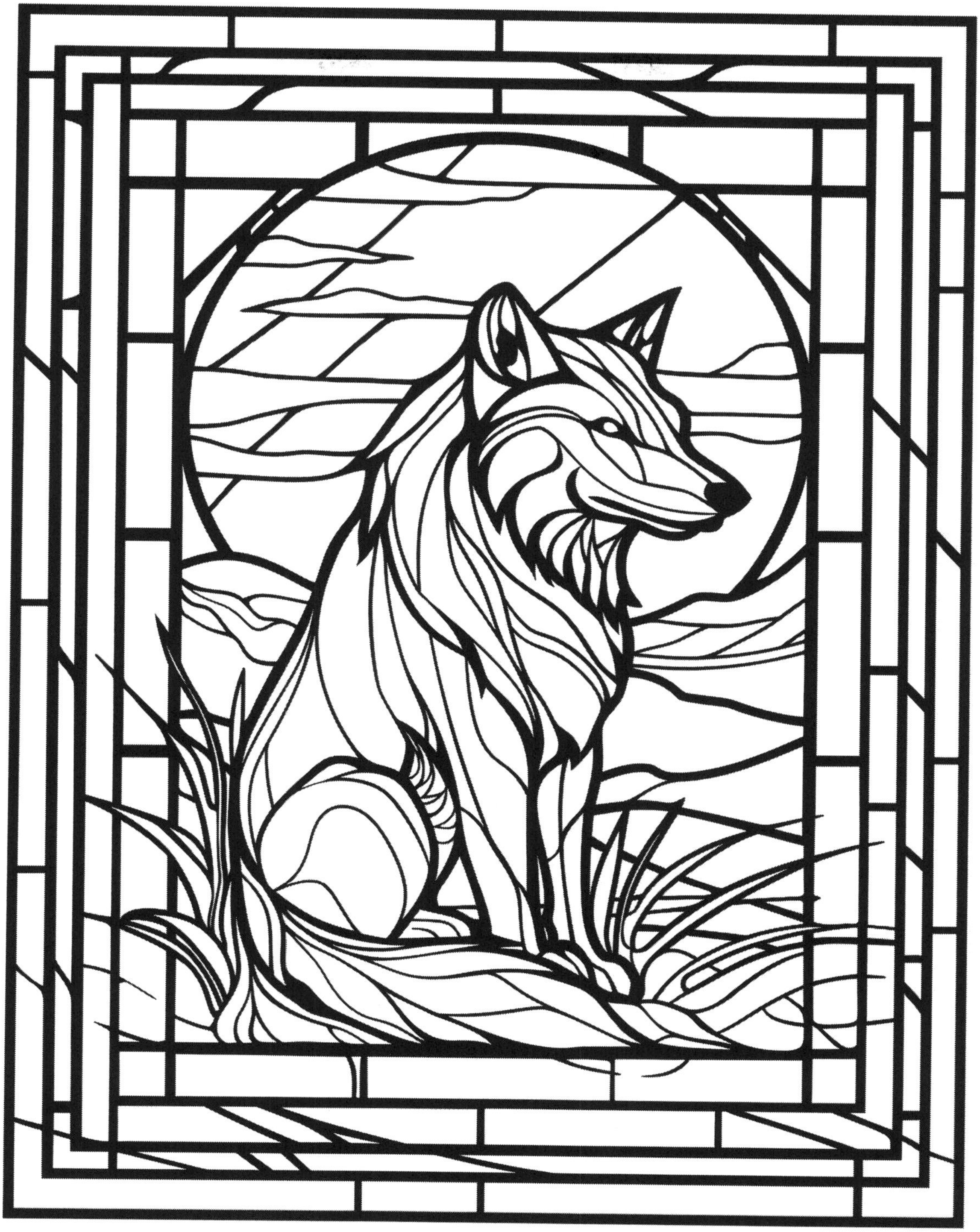

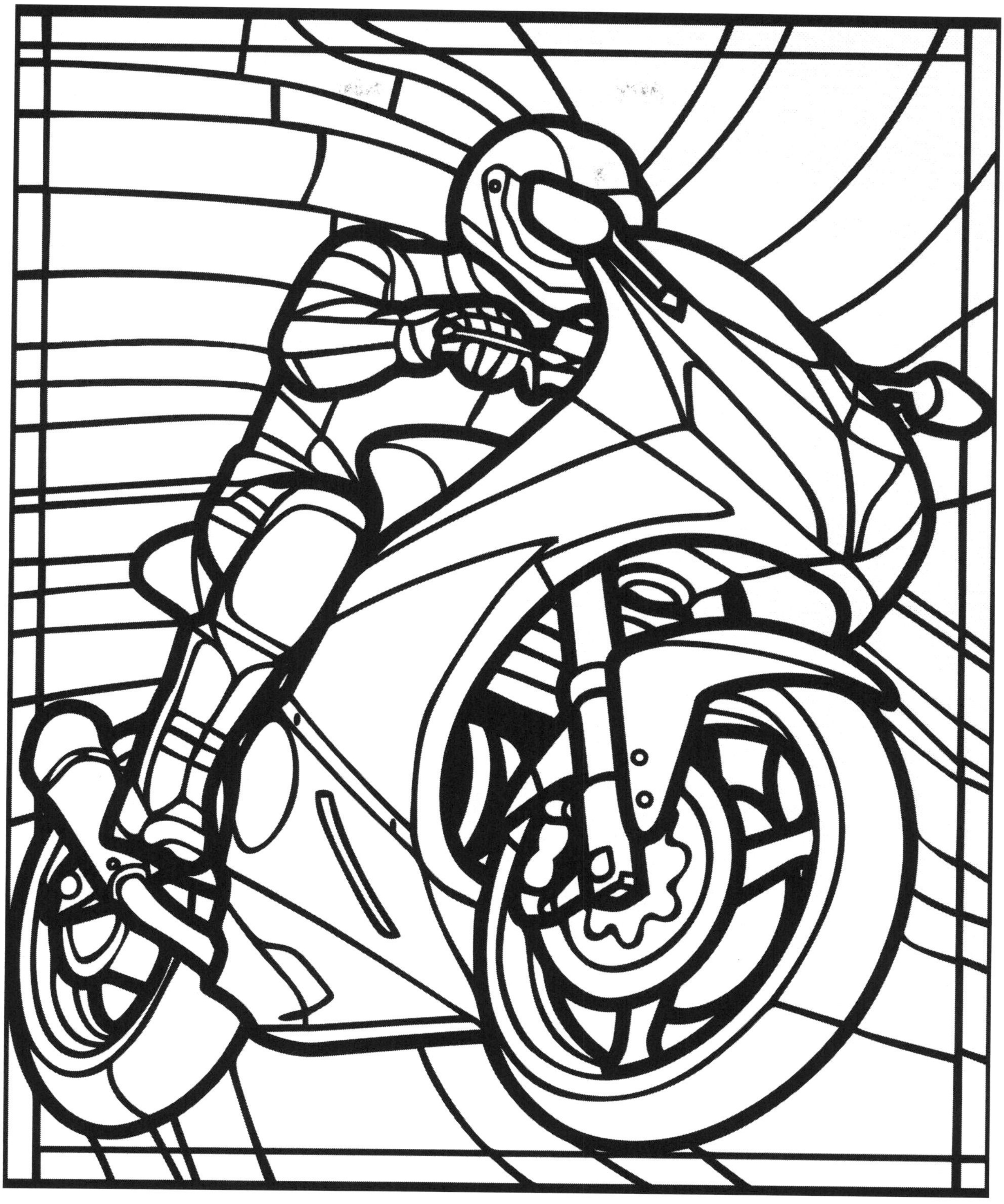

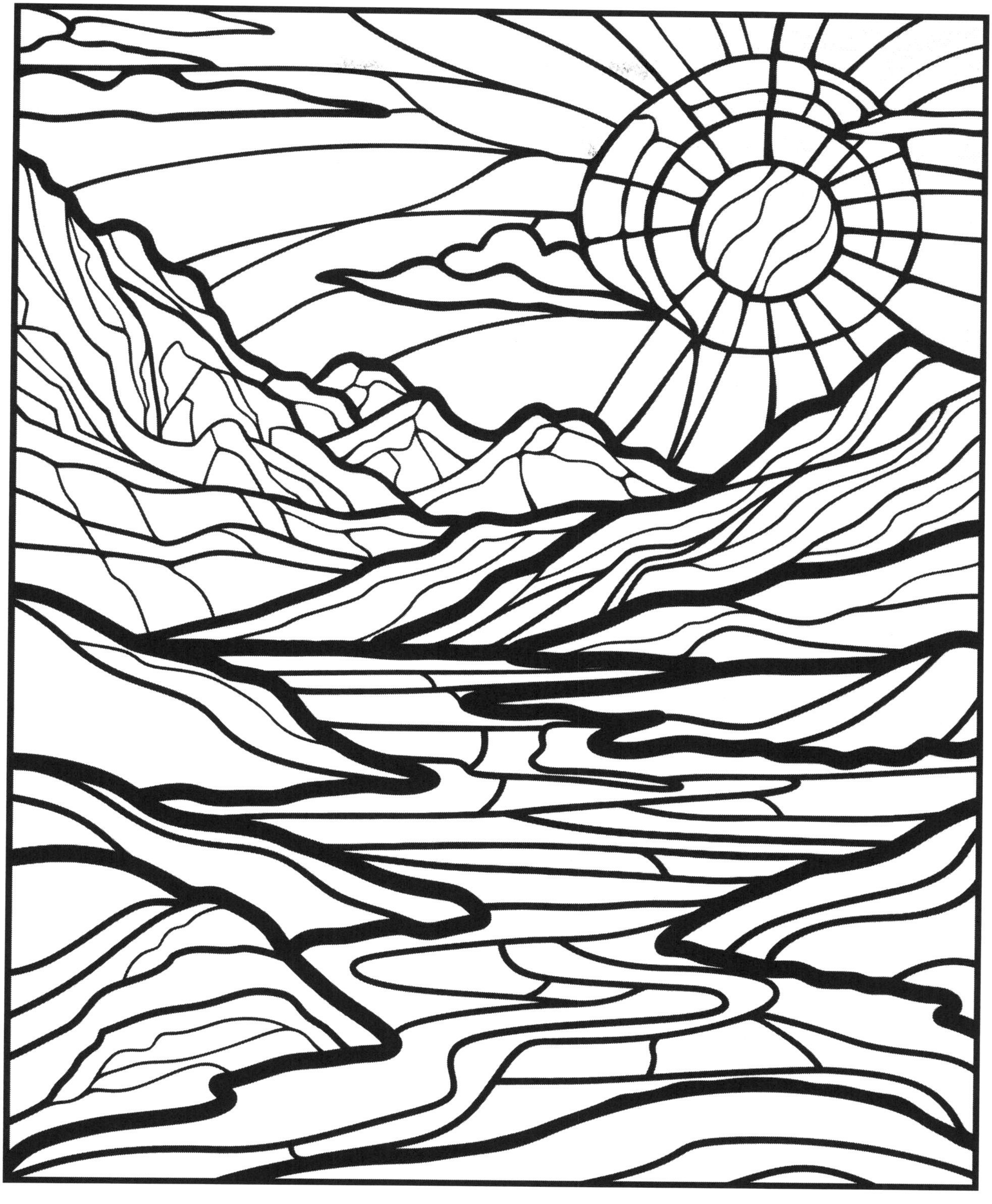

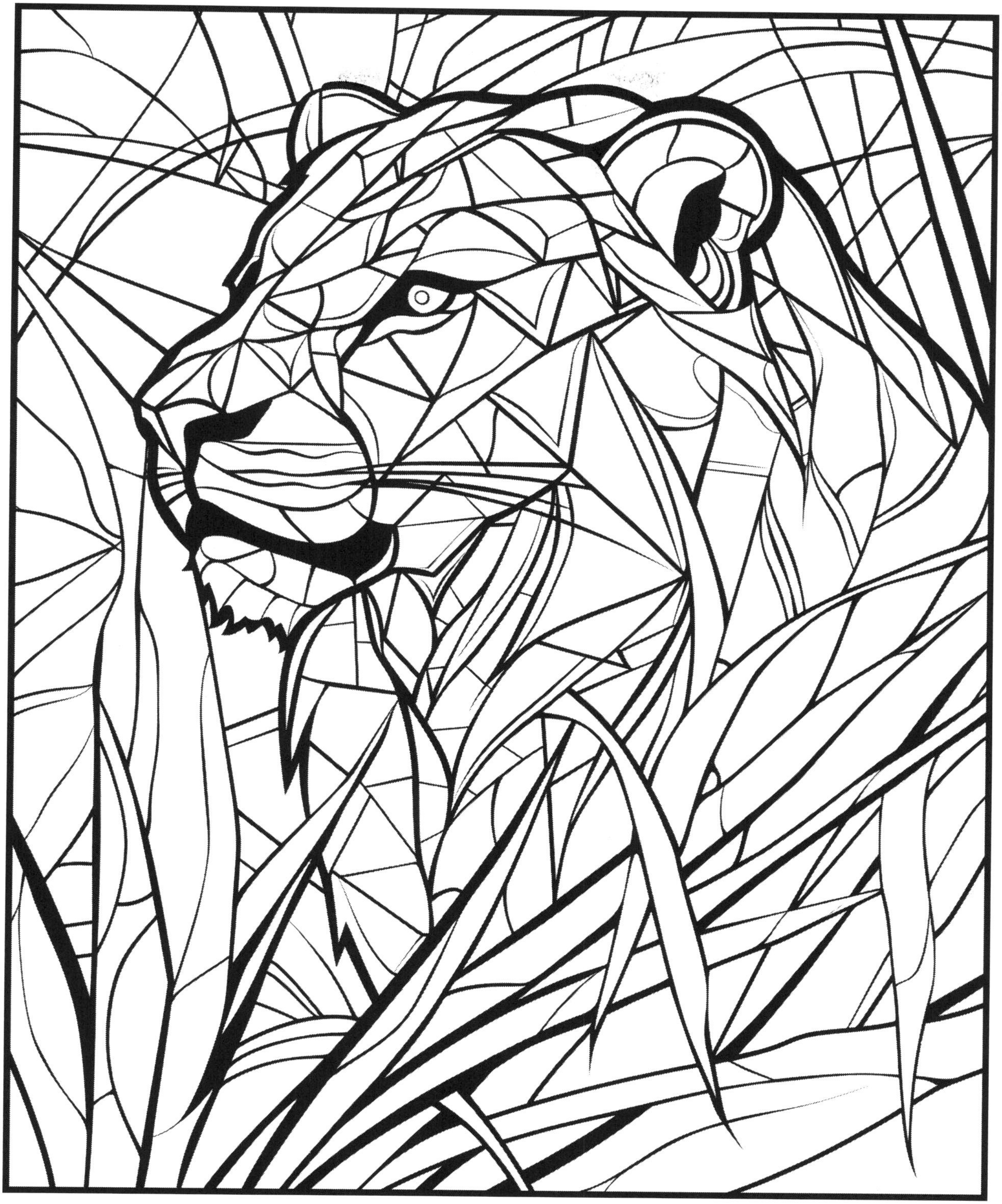

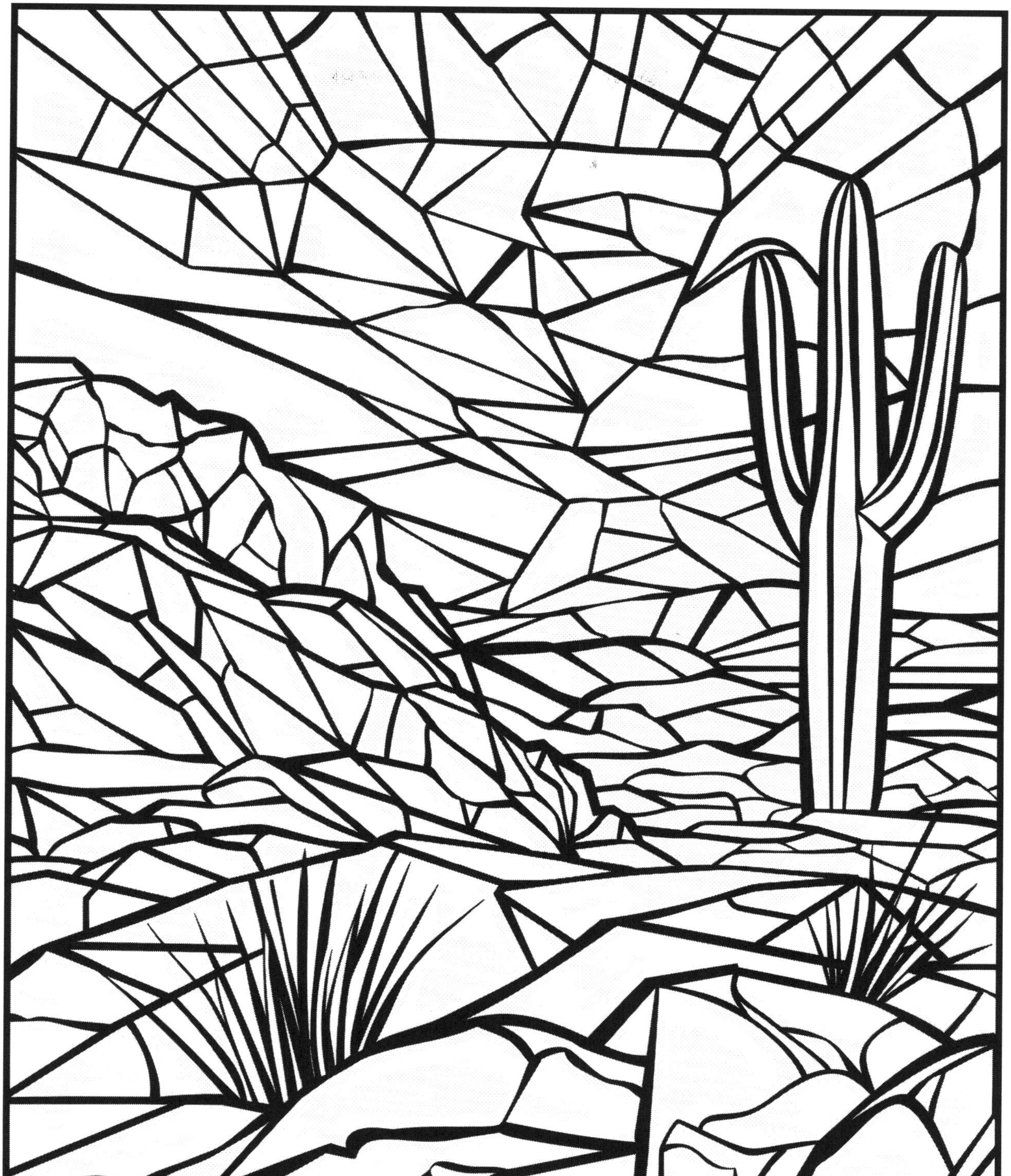

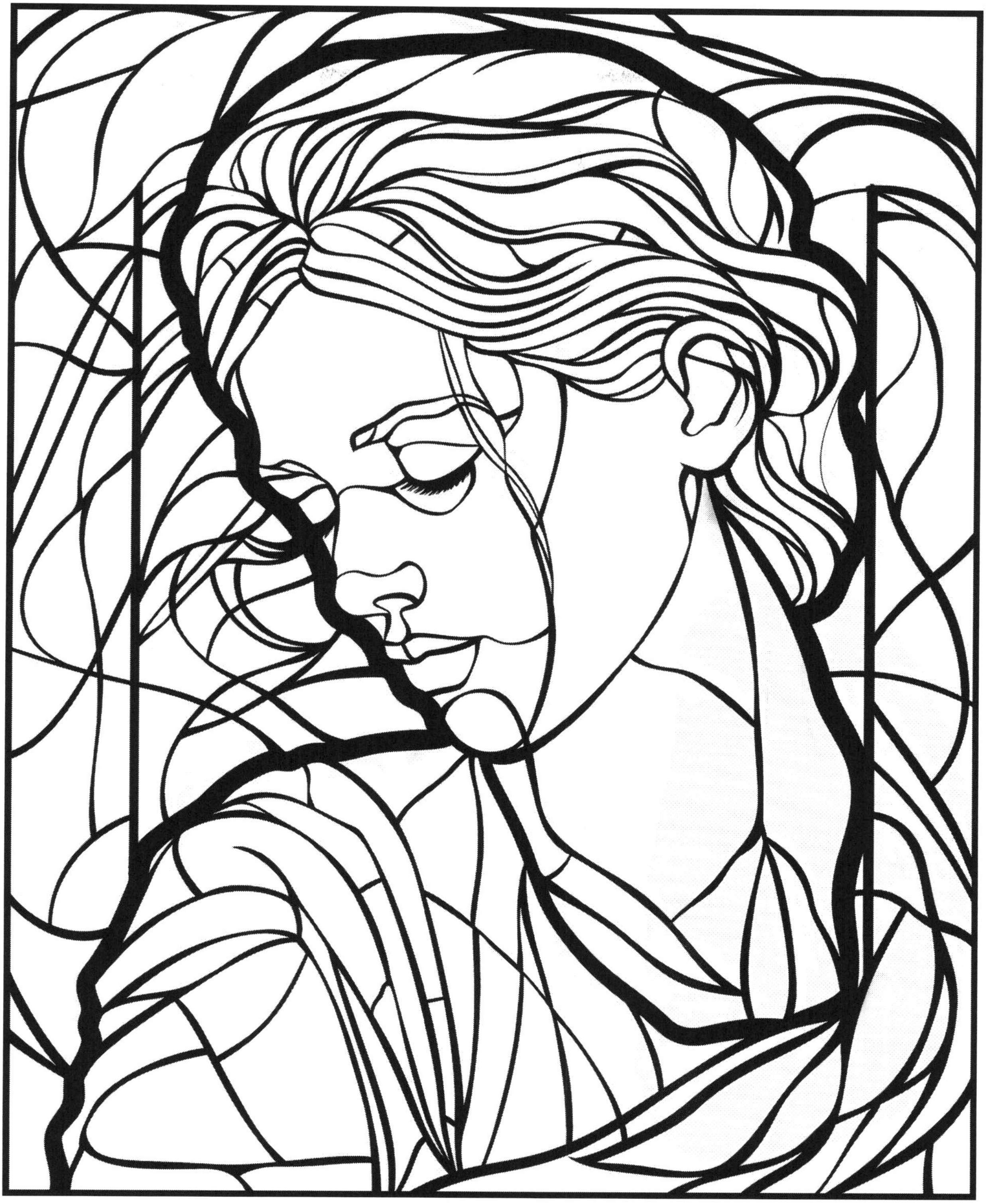

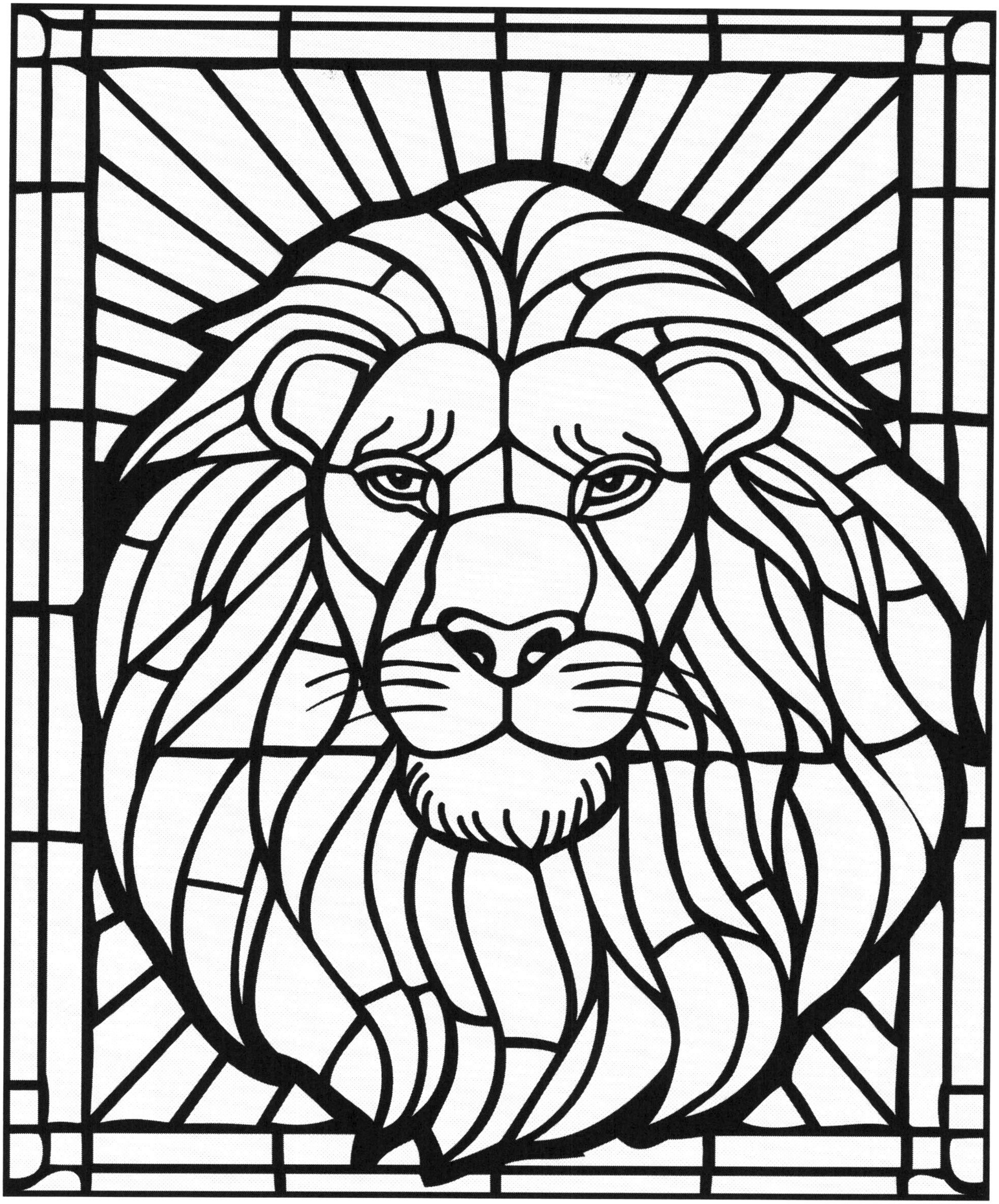

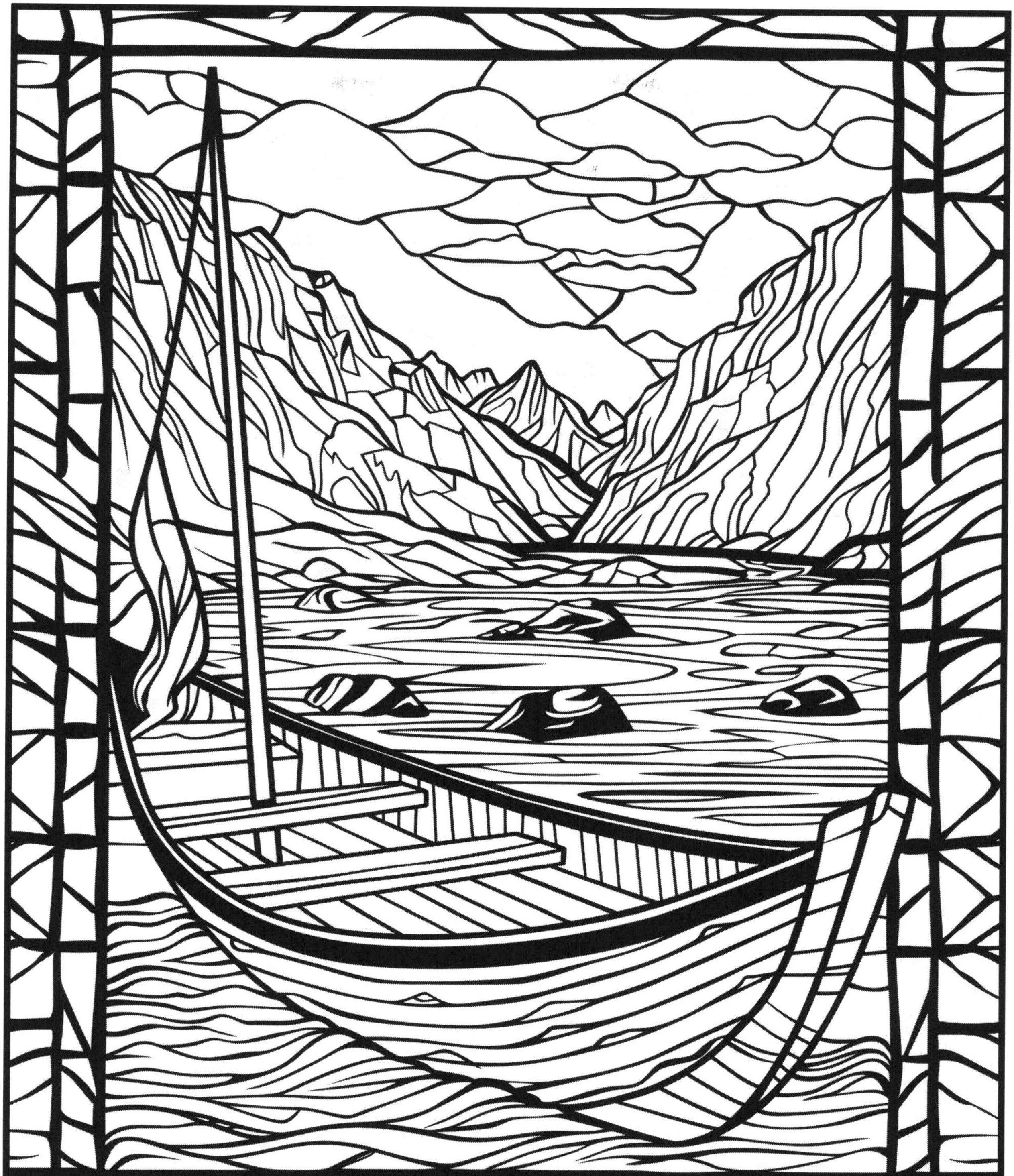

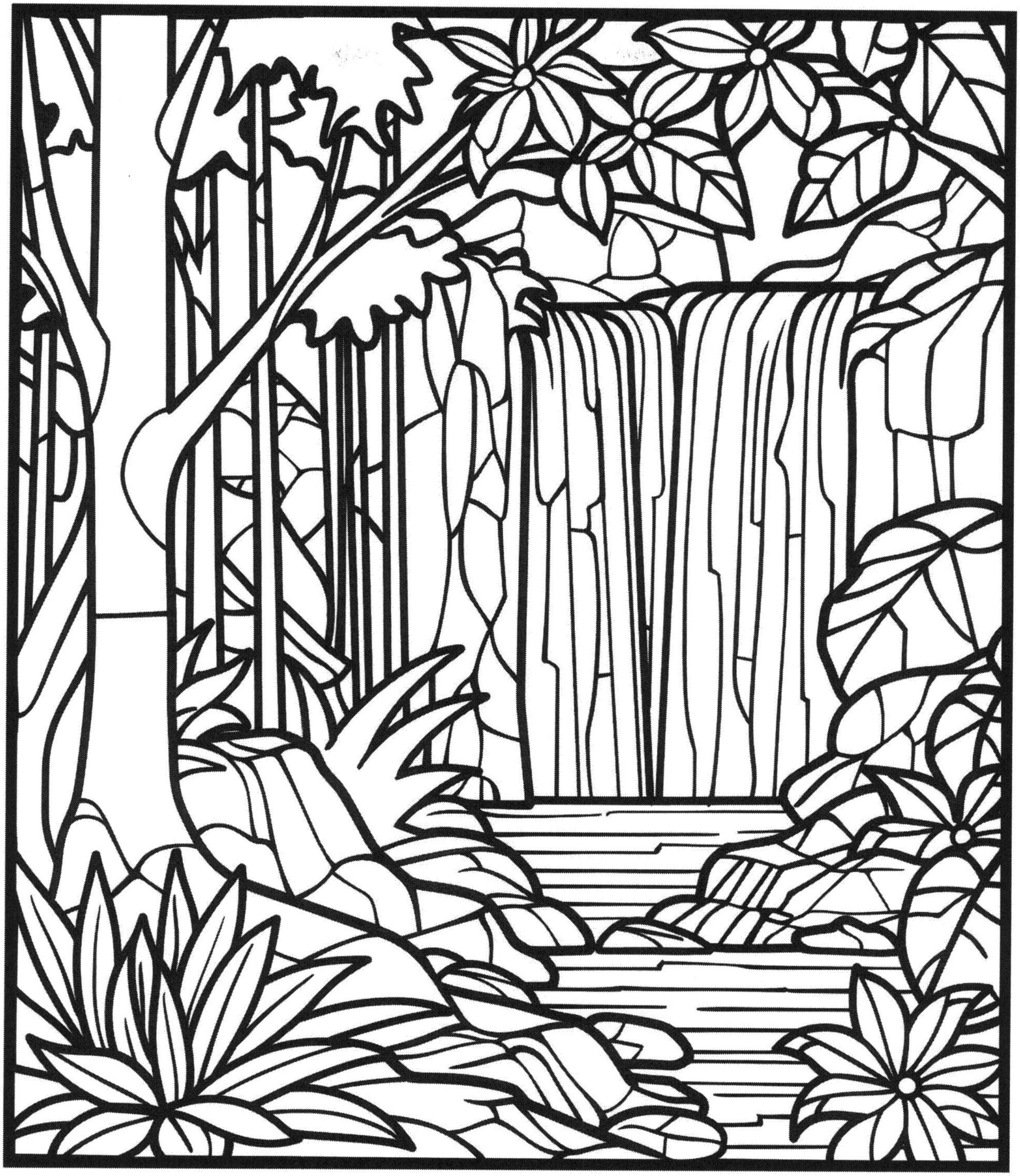

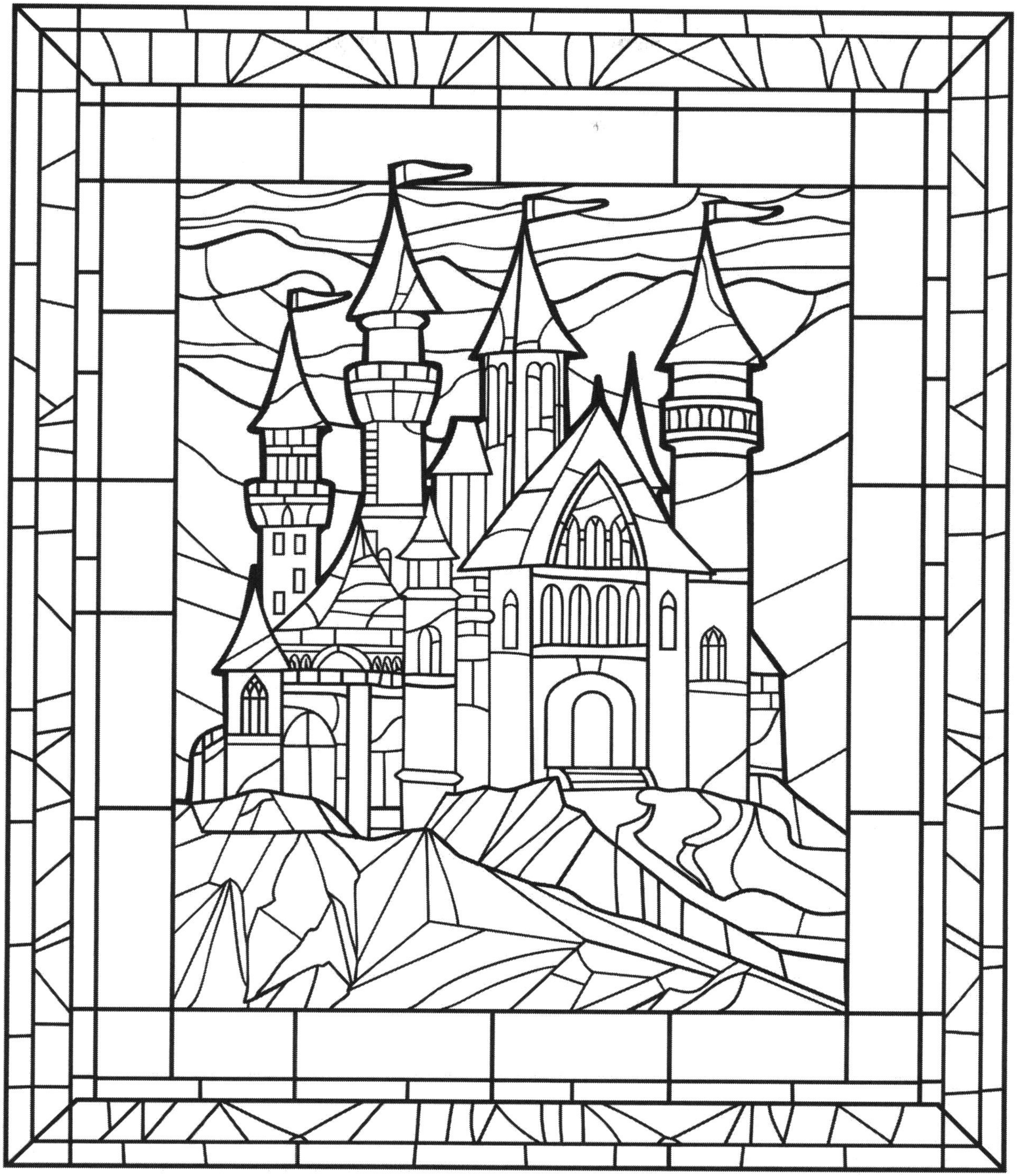

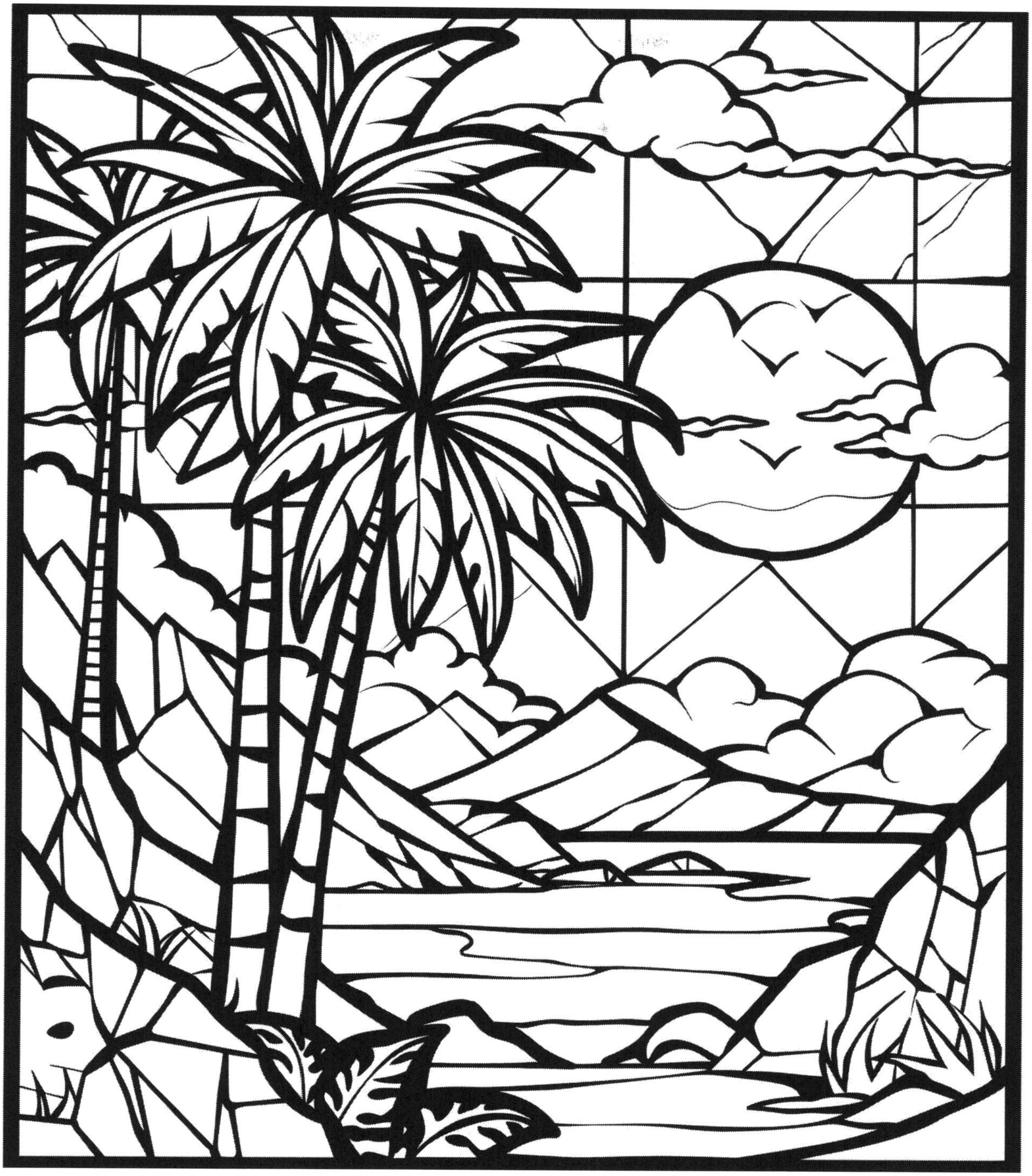

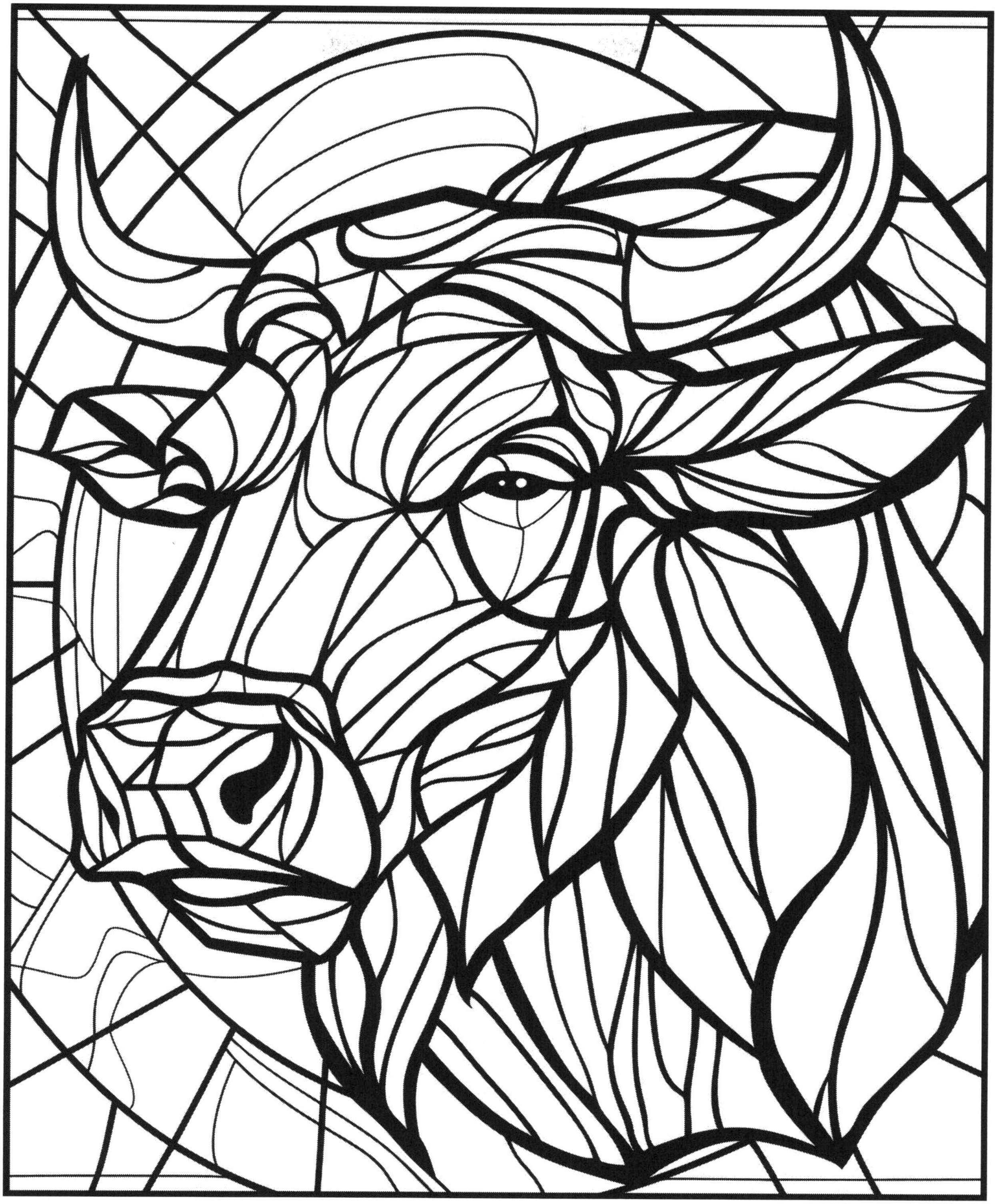

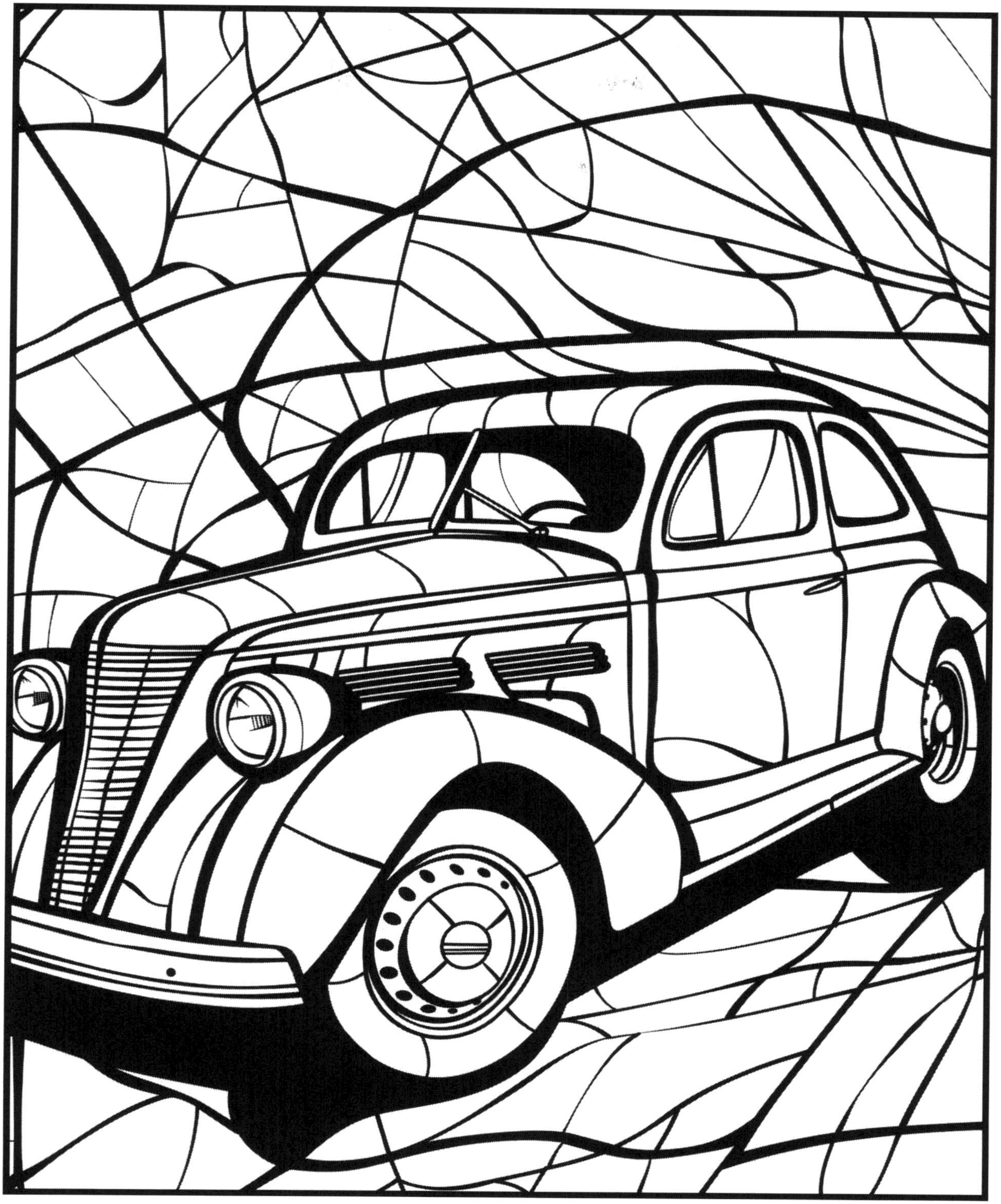

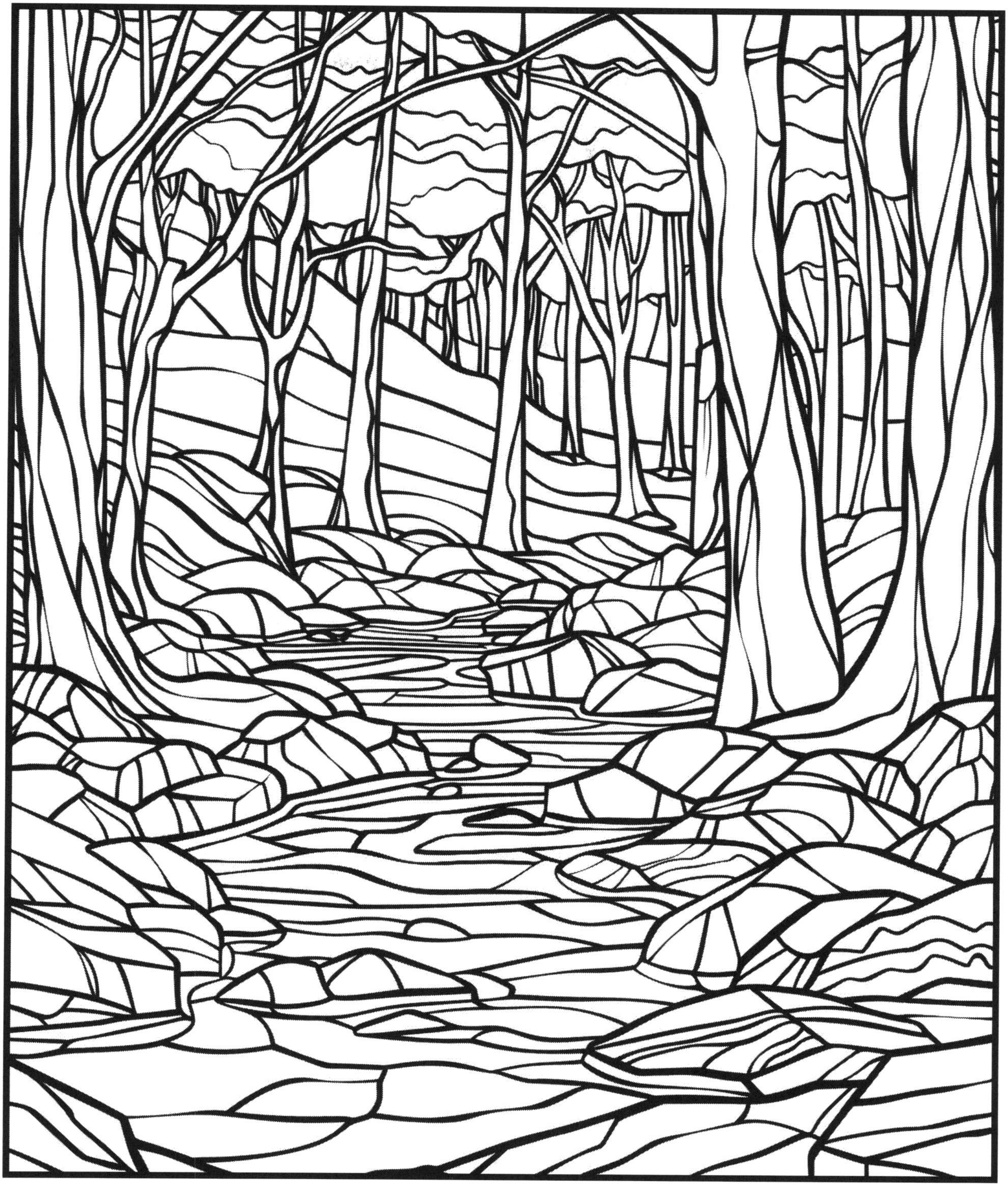

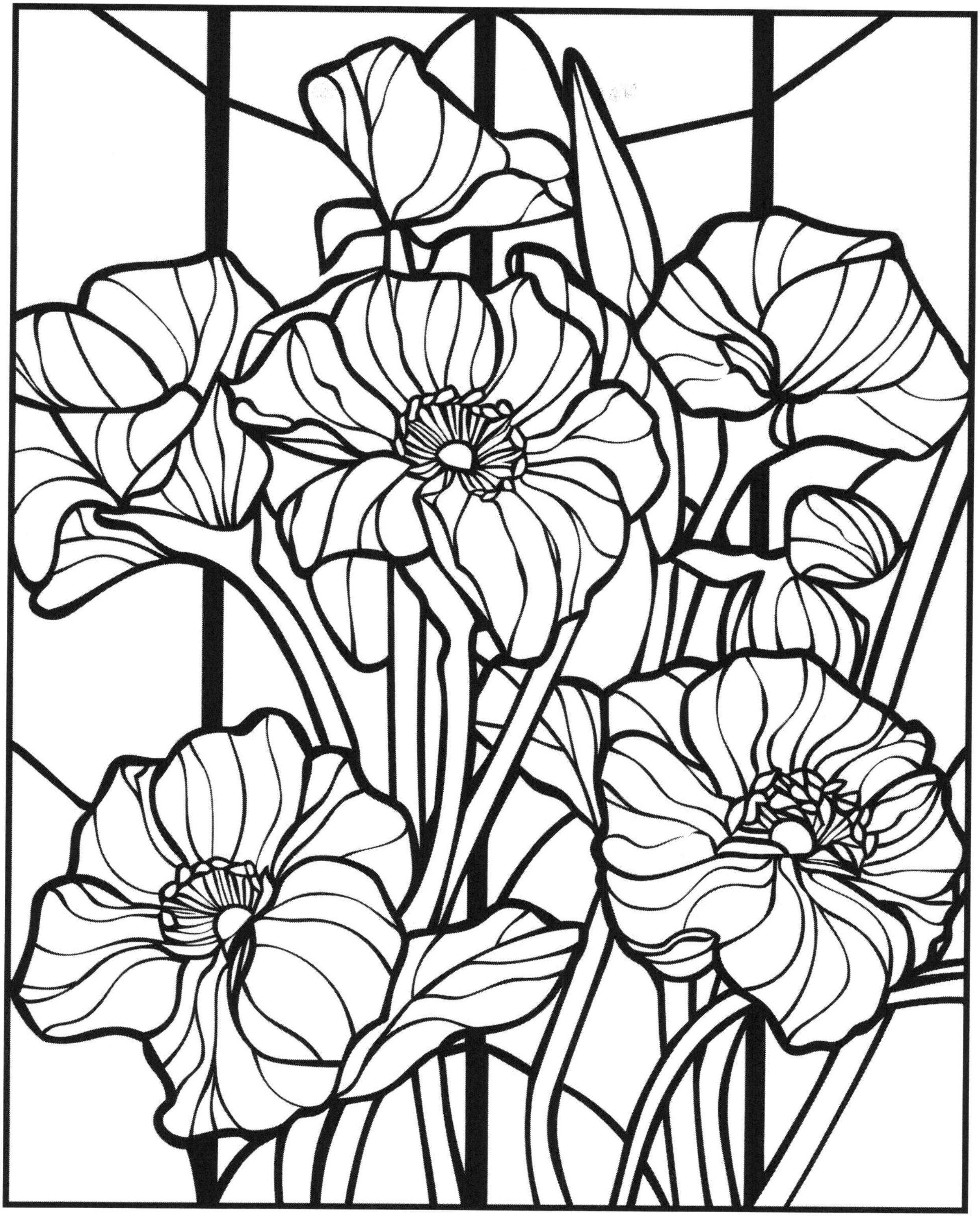

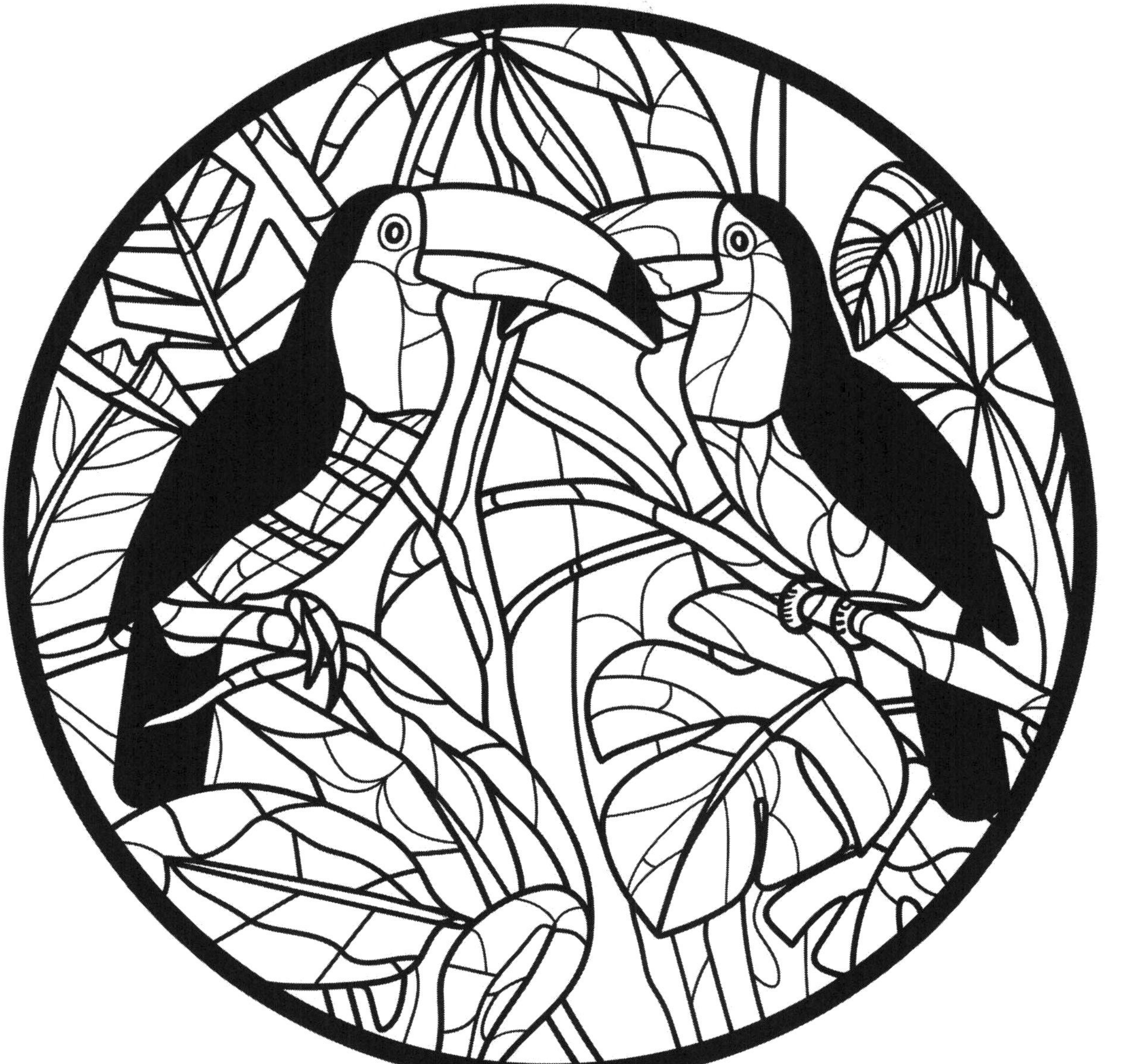

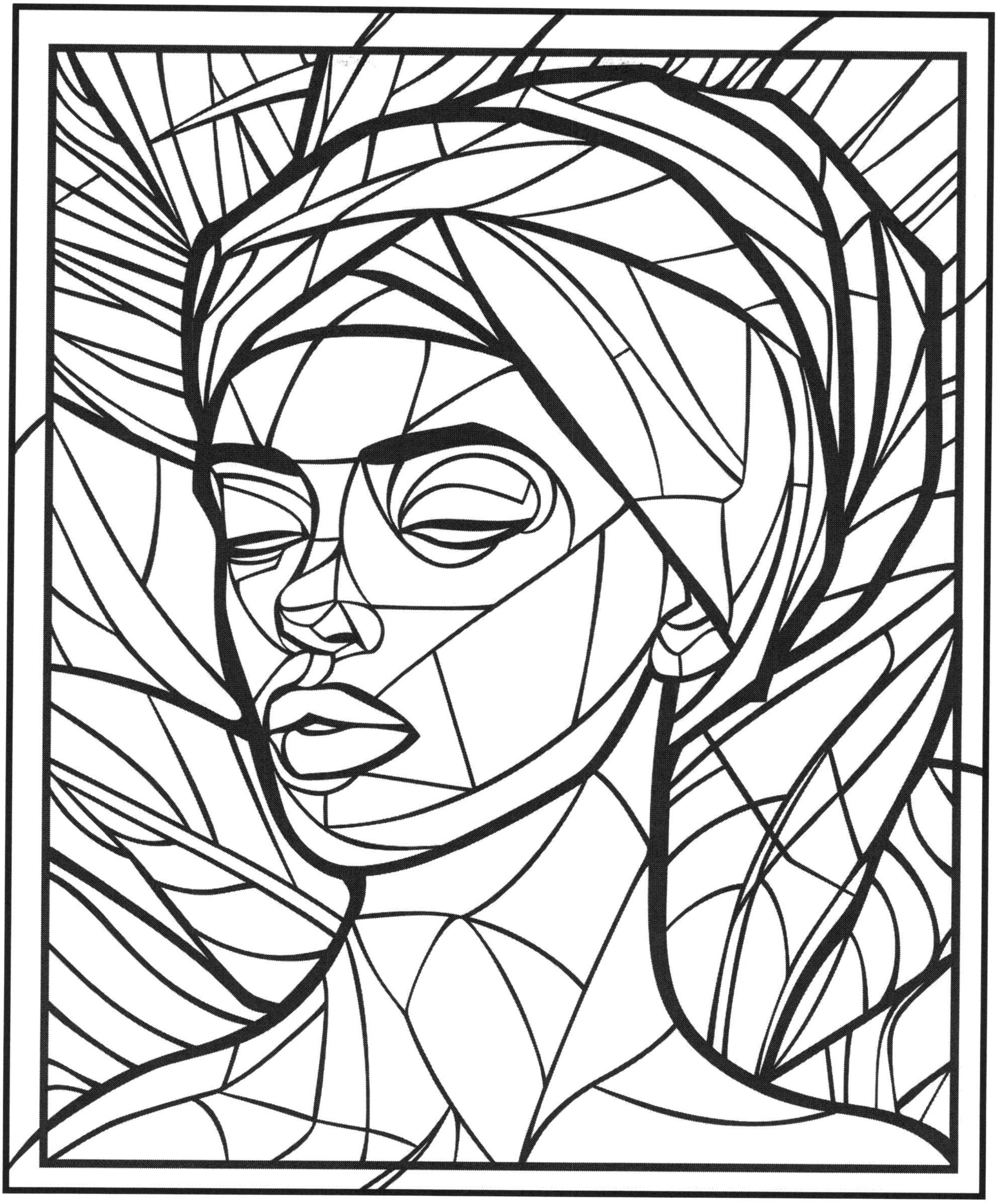

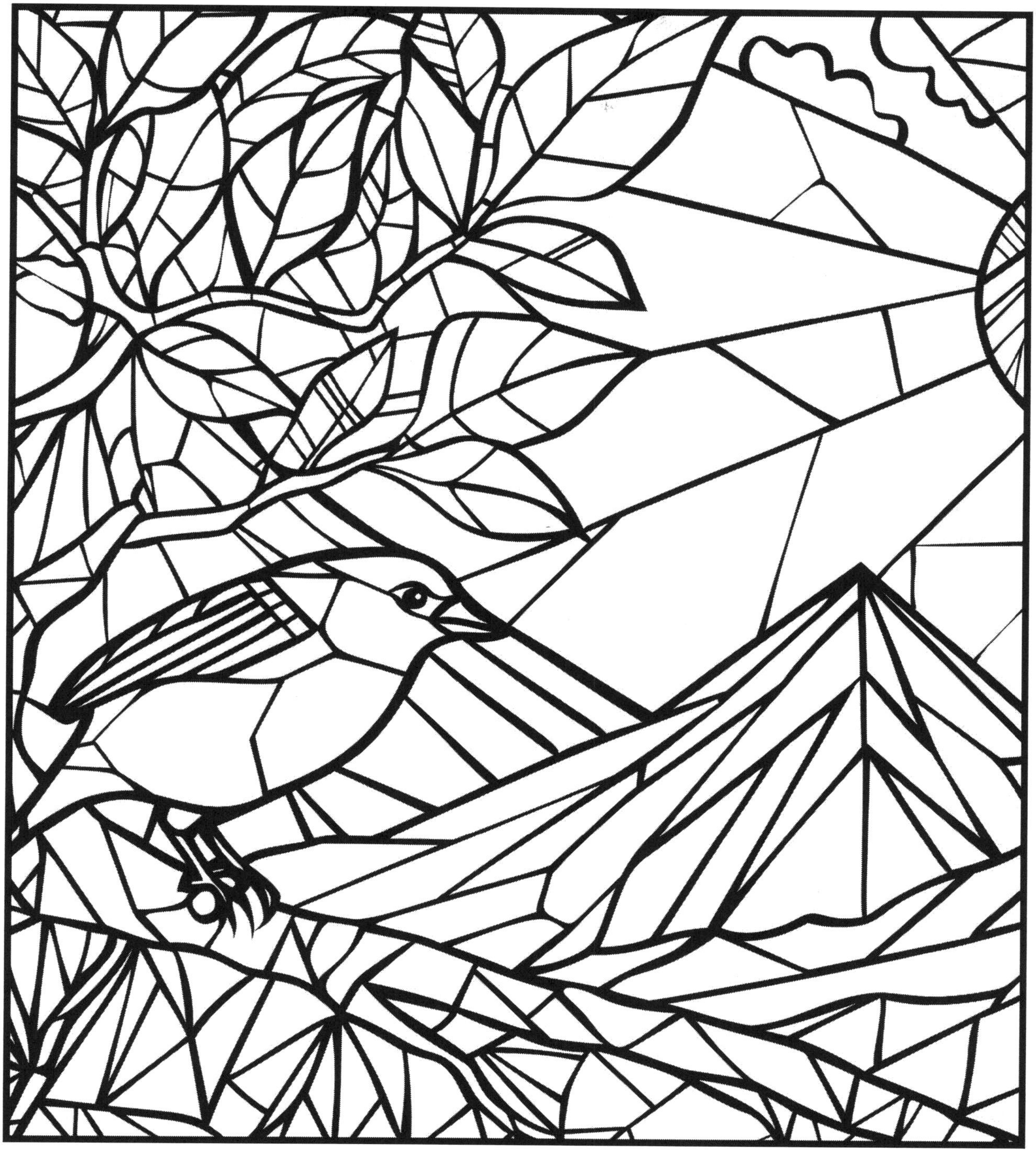

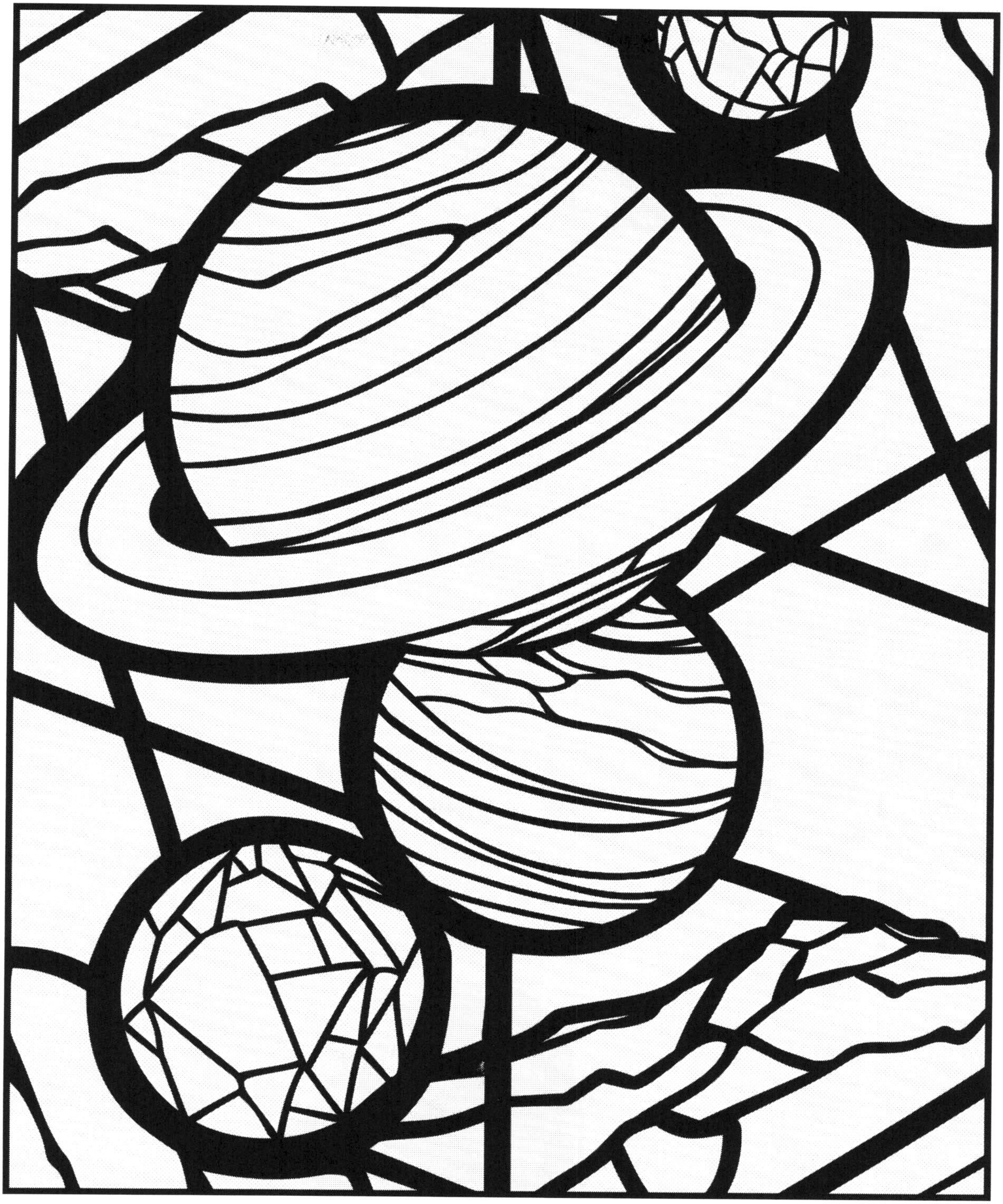

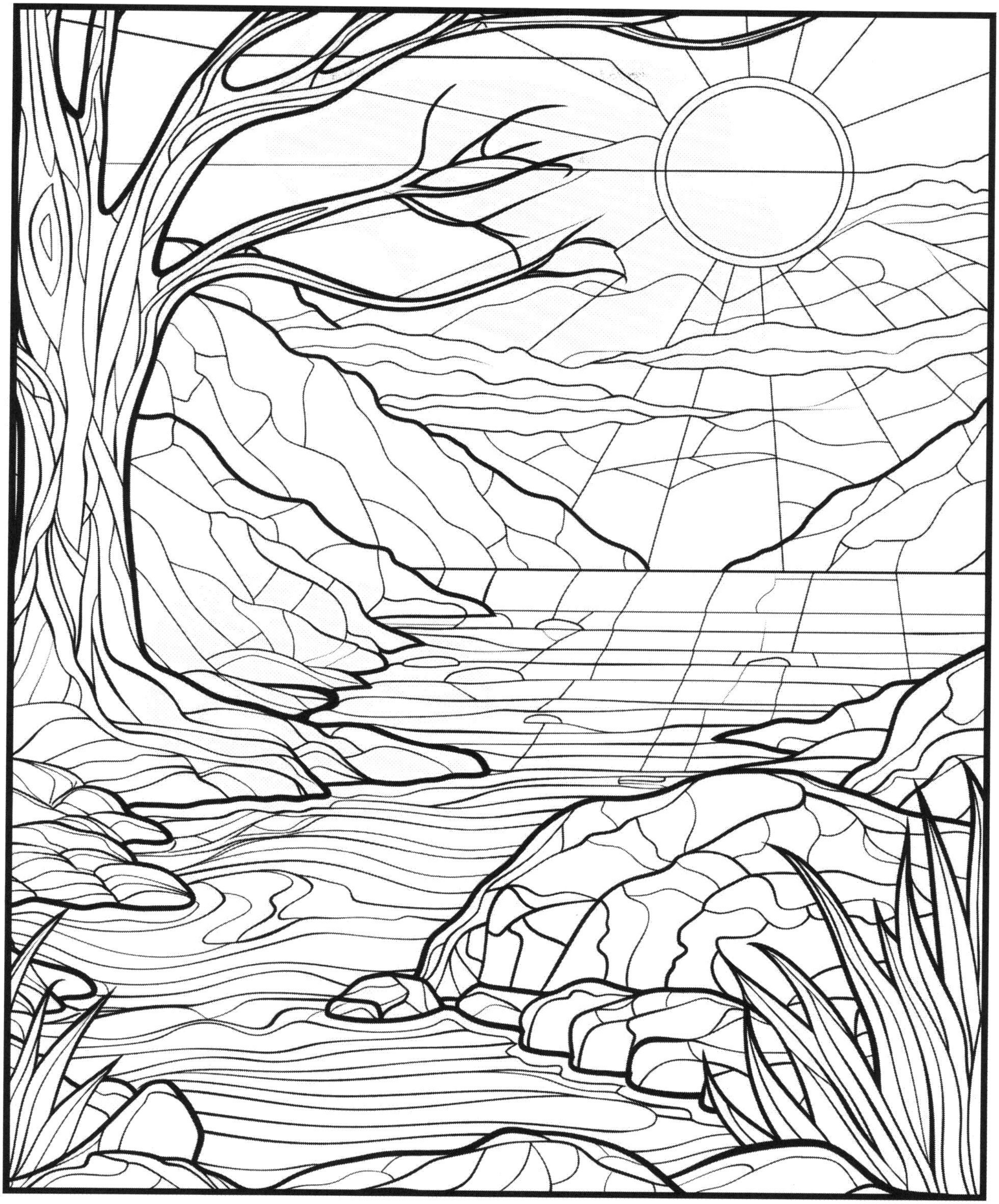

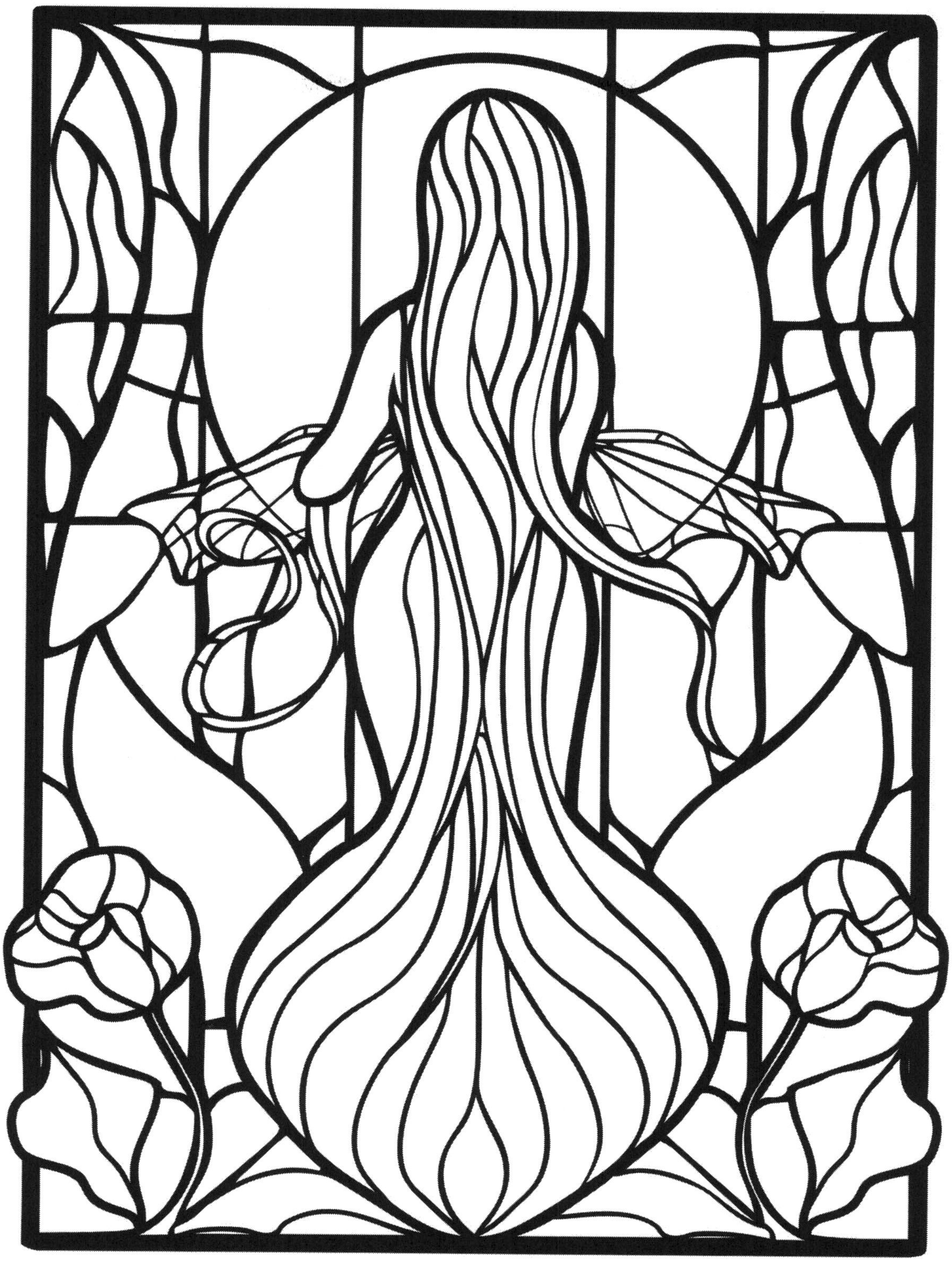

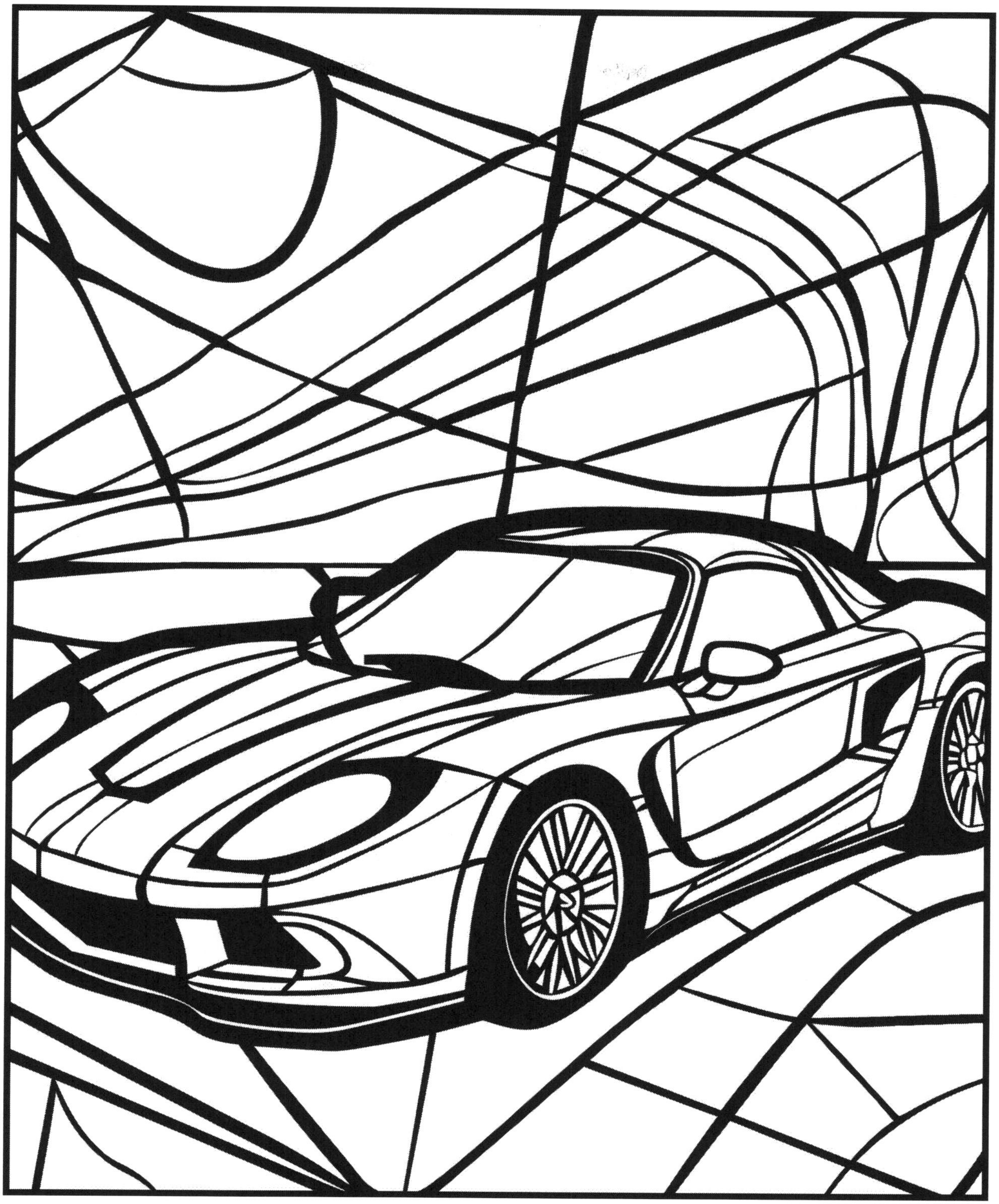

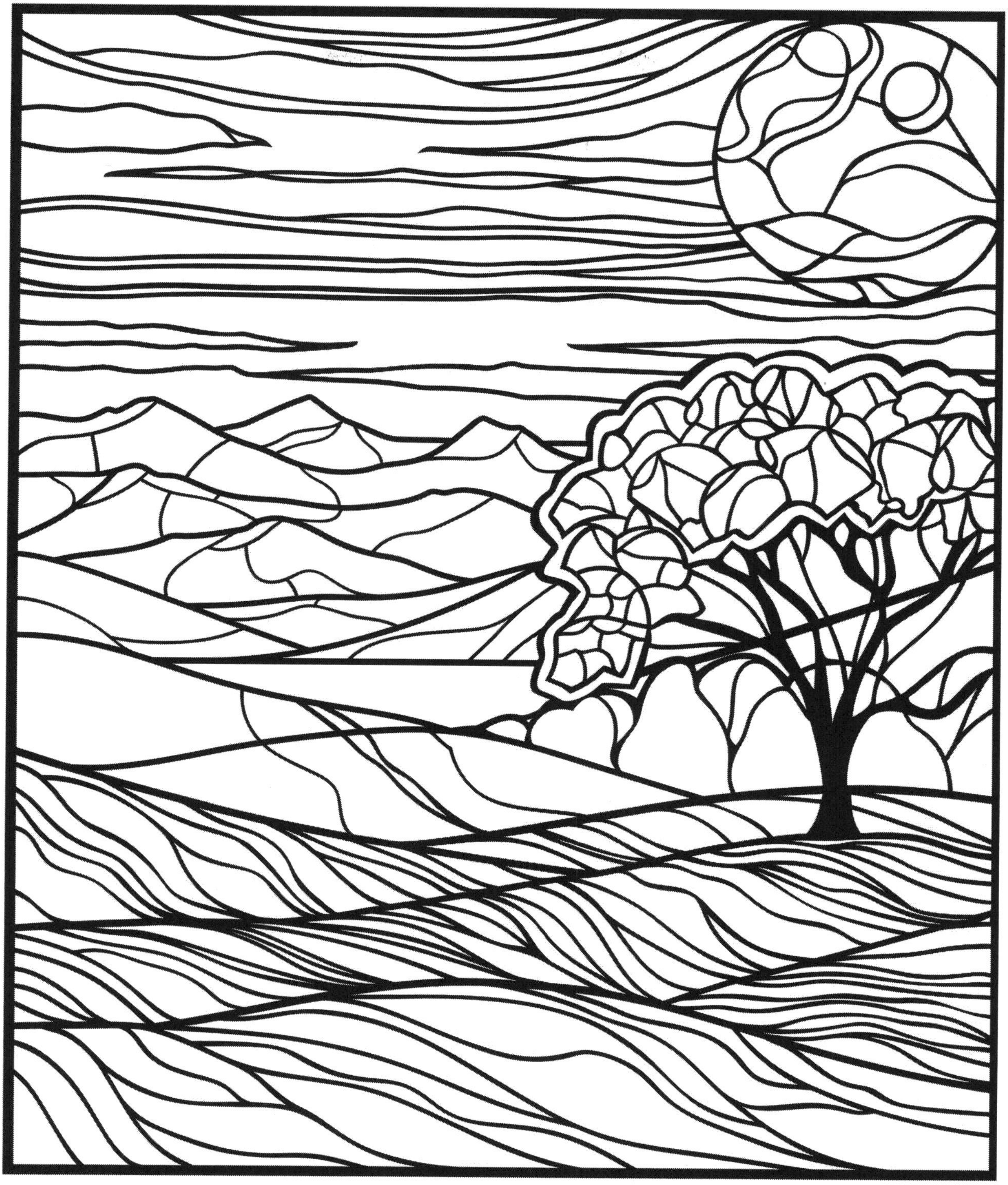

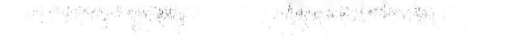

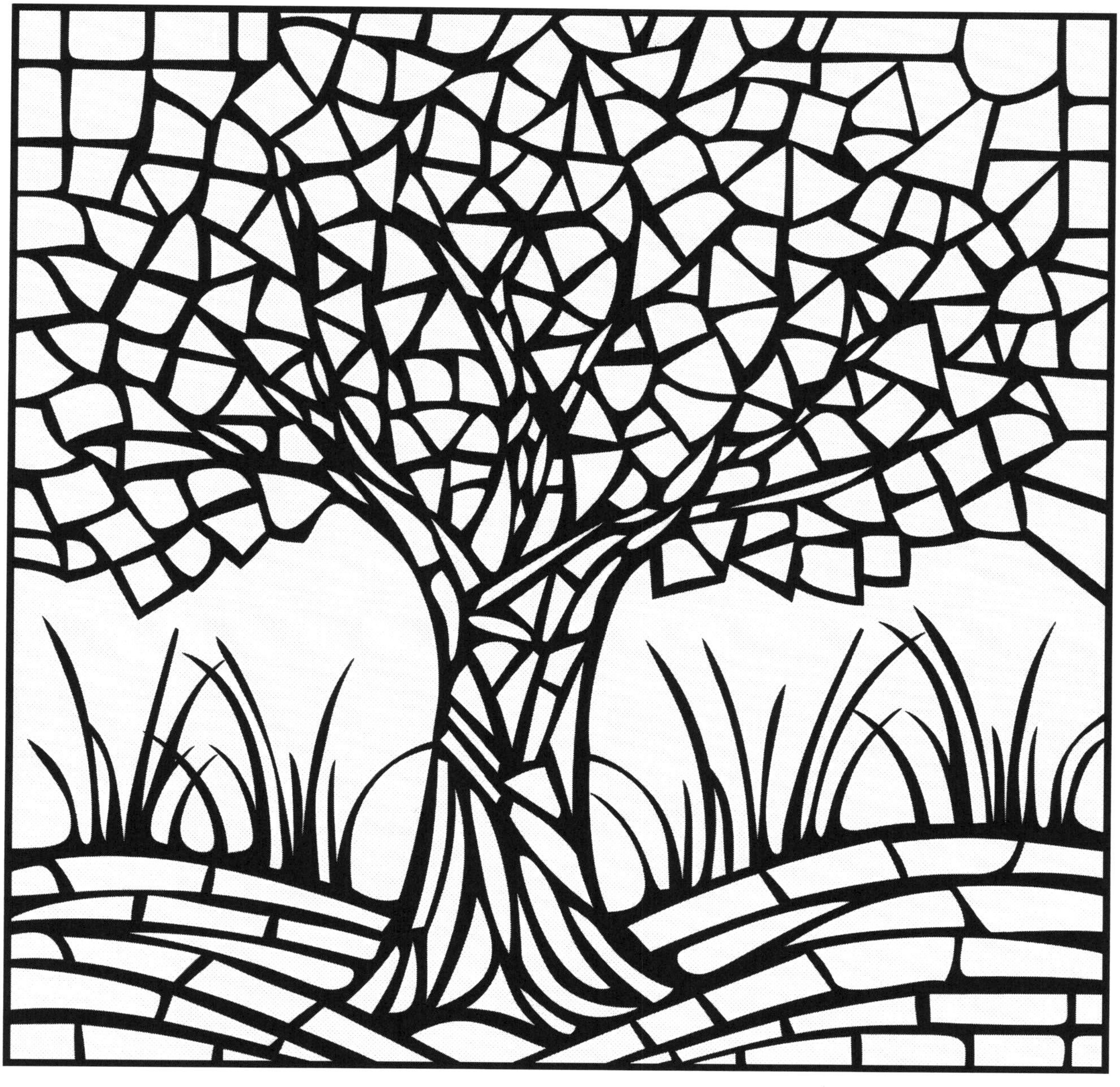

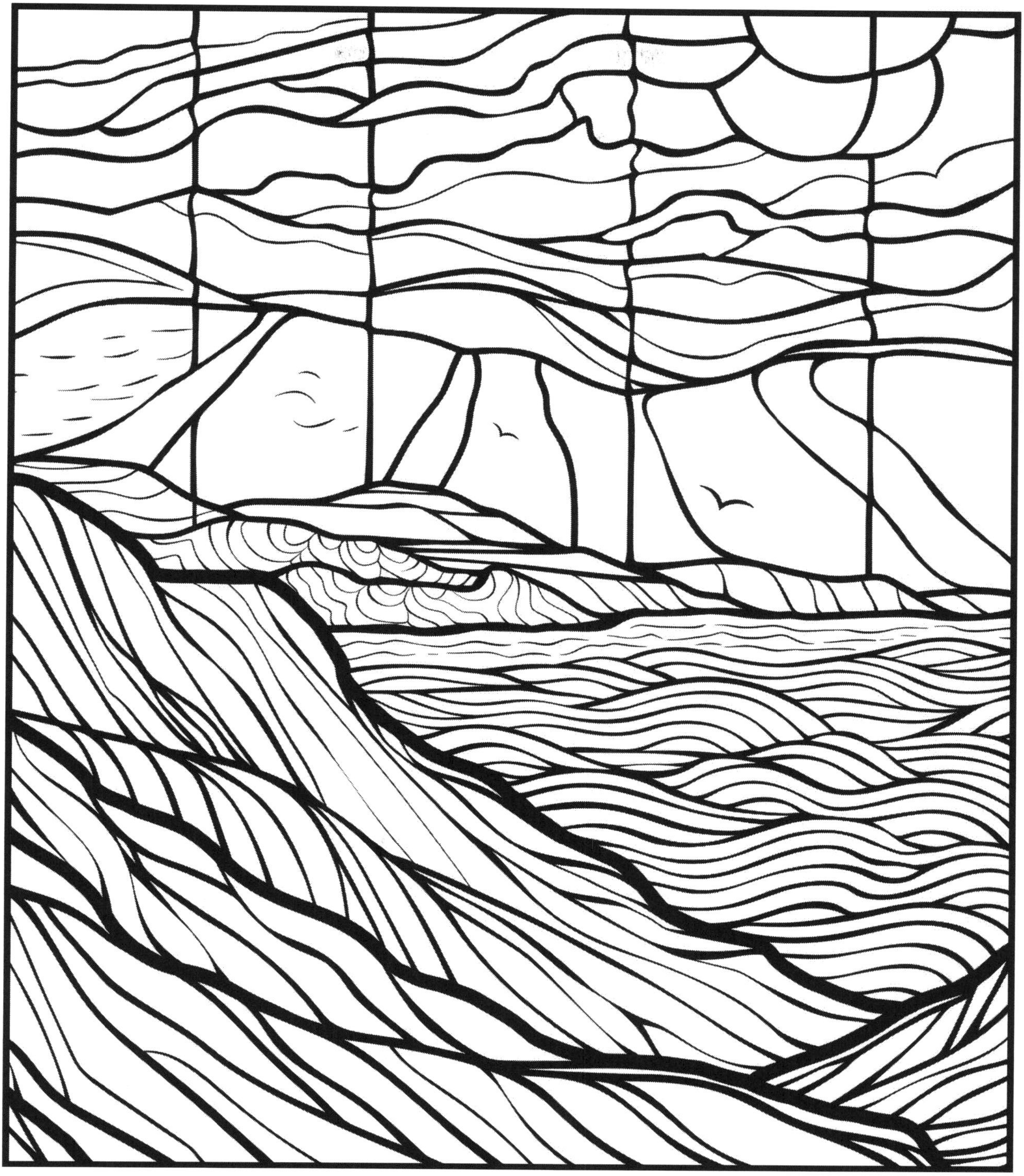

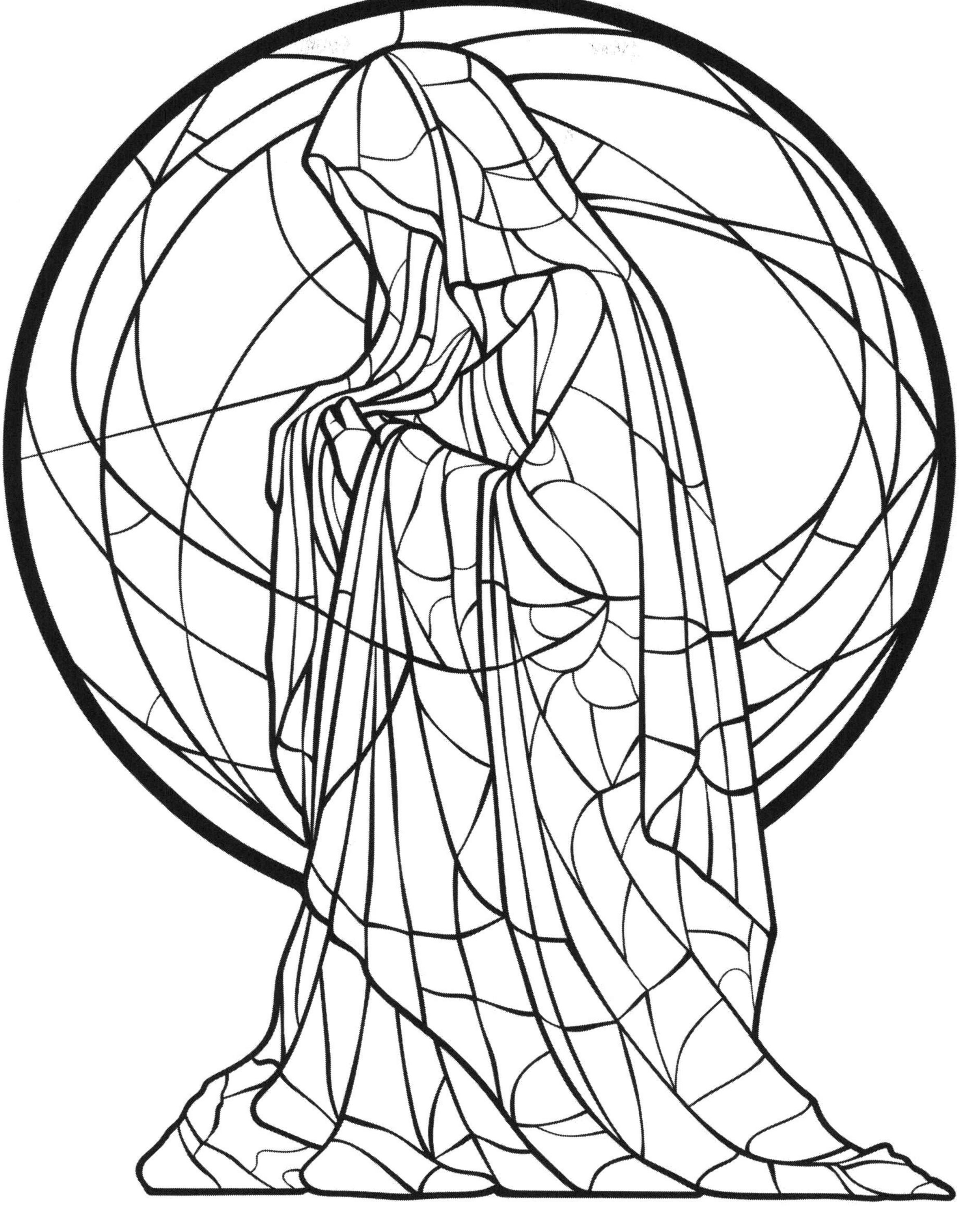

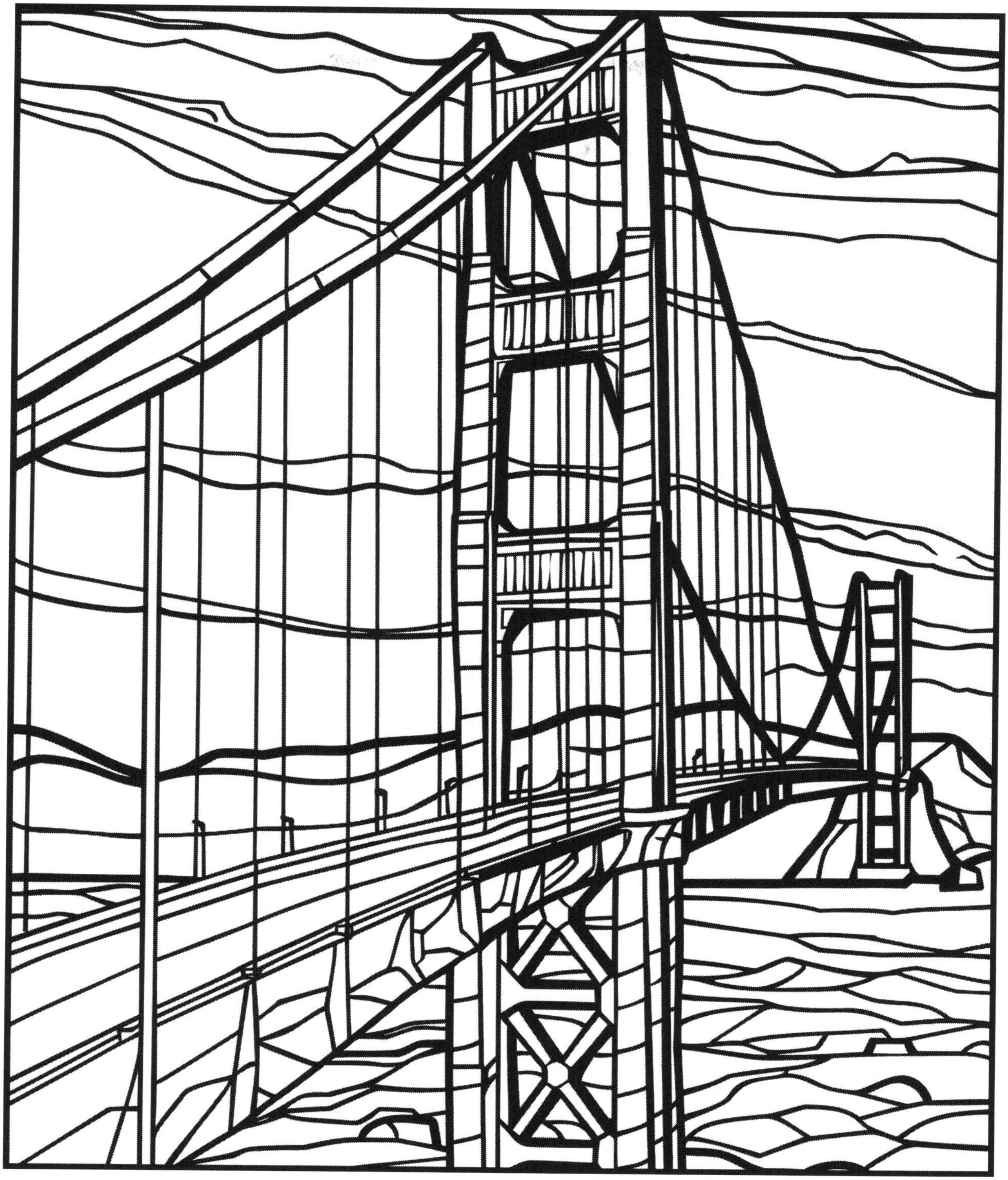

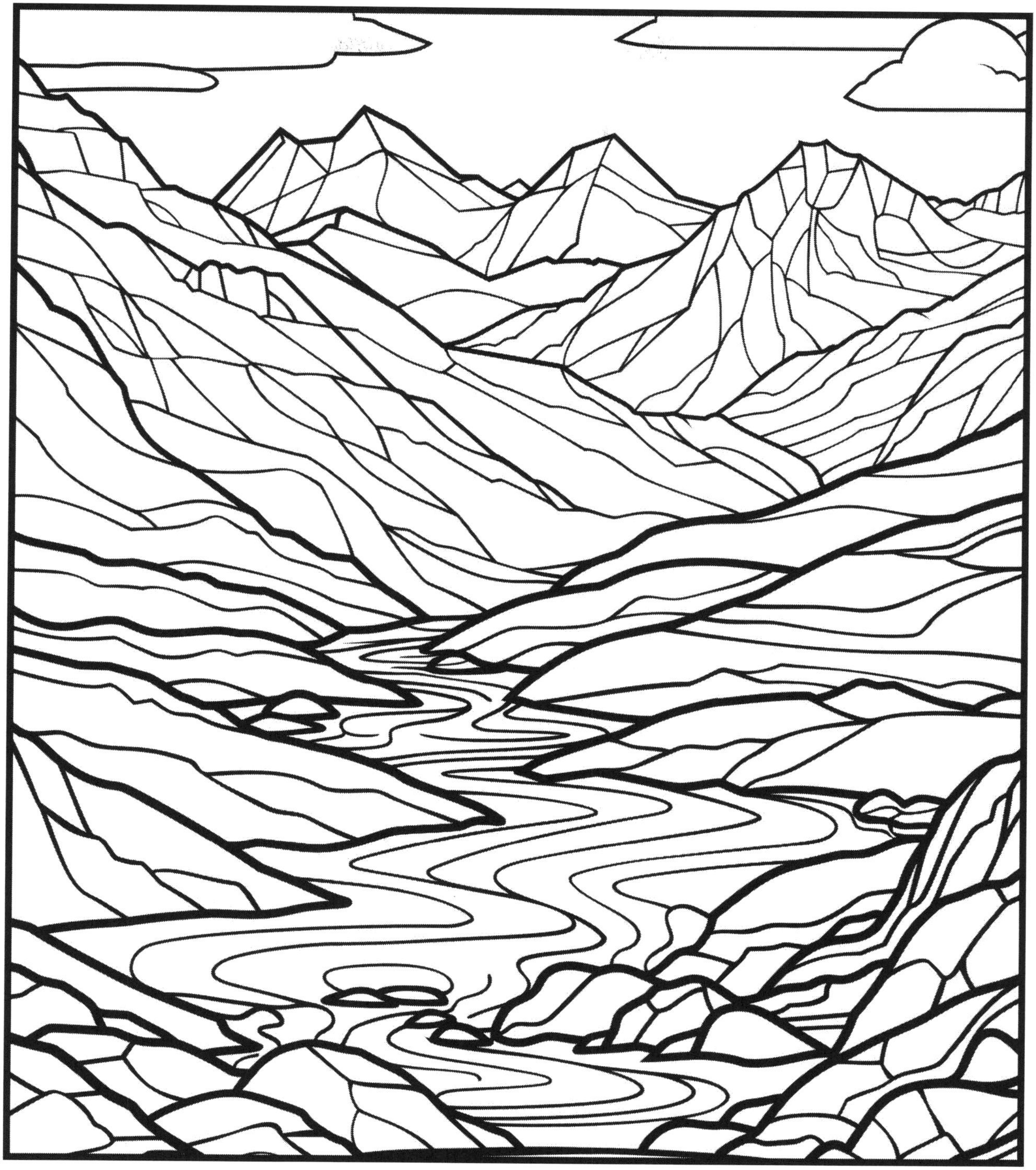

thank you

so much for purchasing the book! Your support means the world to us. As you journey through the following pages, you'll discover some special surprises and gifts awaiting you. I hope they bring you joy and enrich your coloring experience. Happy exploring!
Colorful Paint

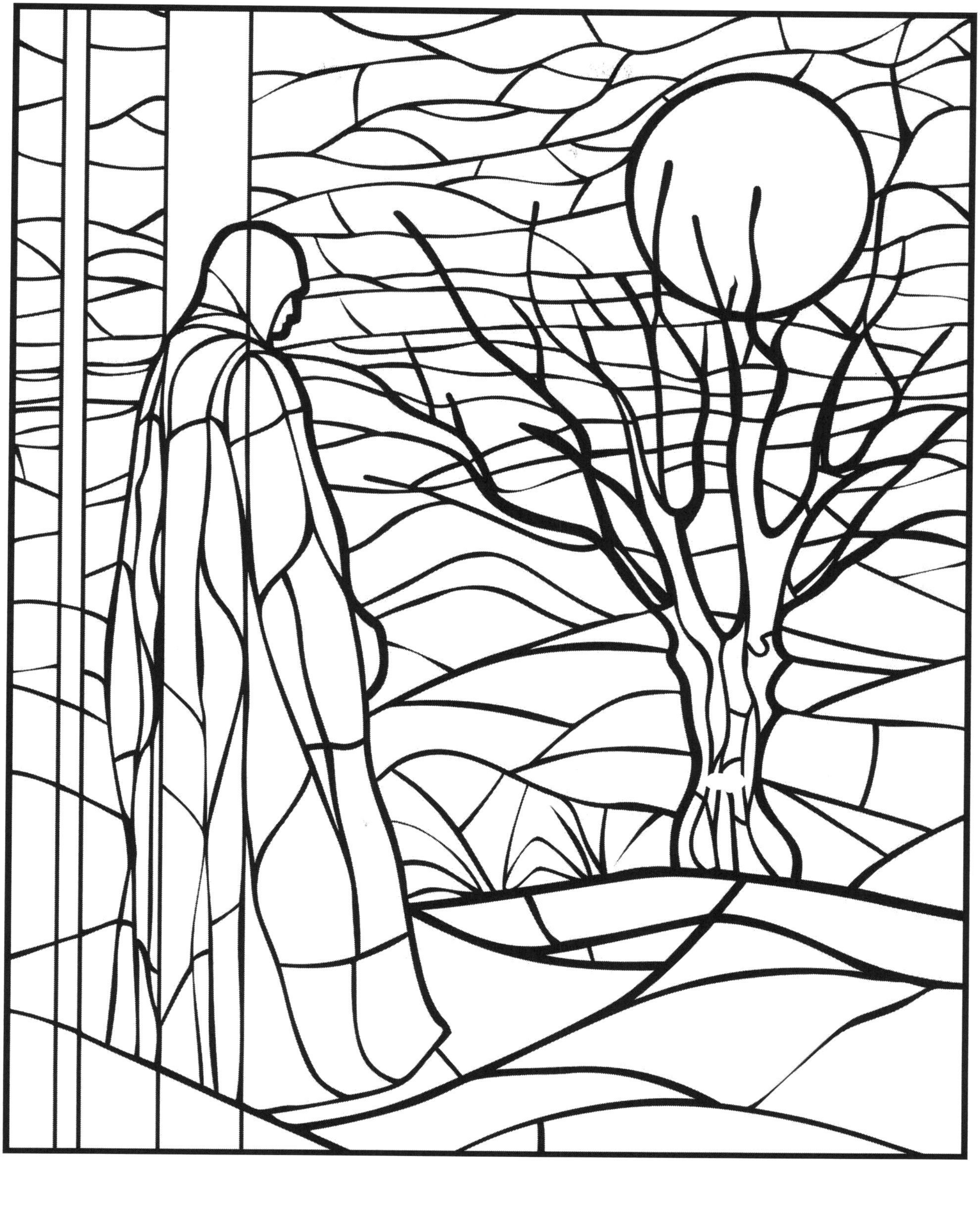

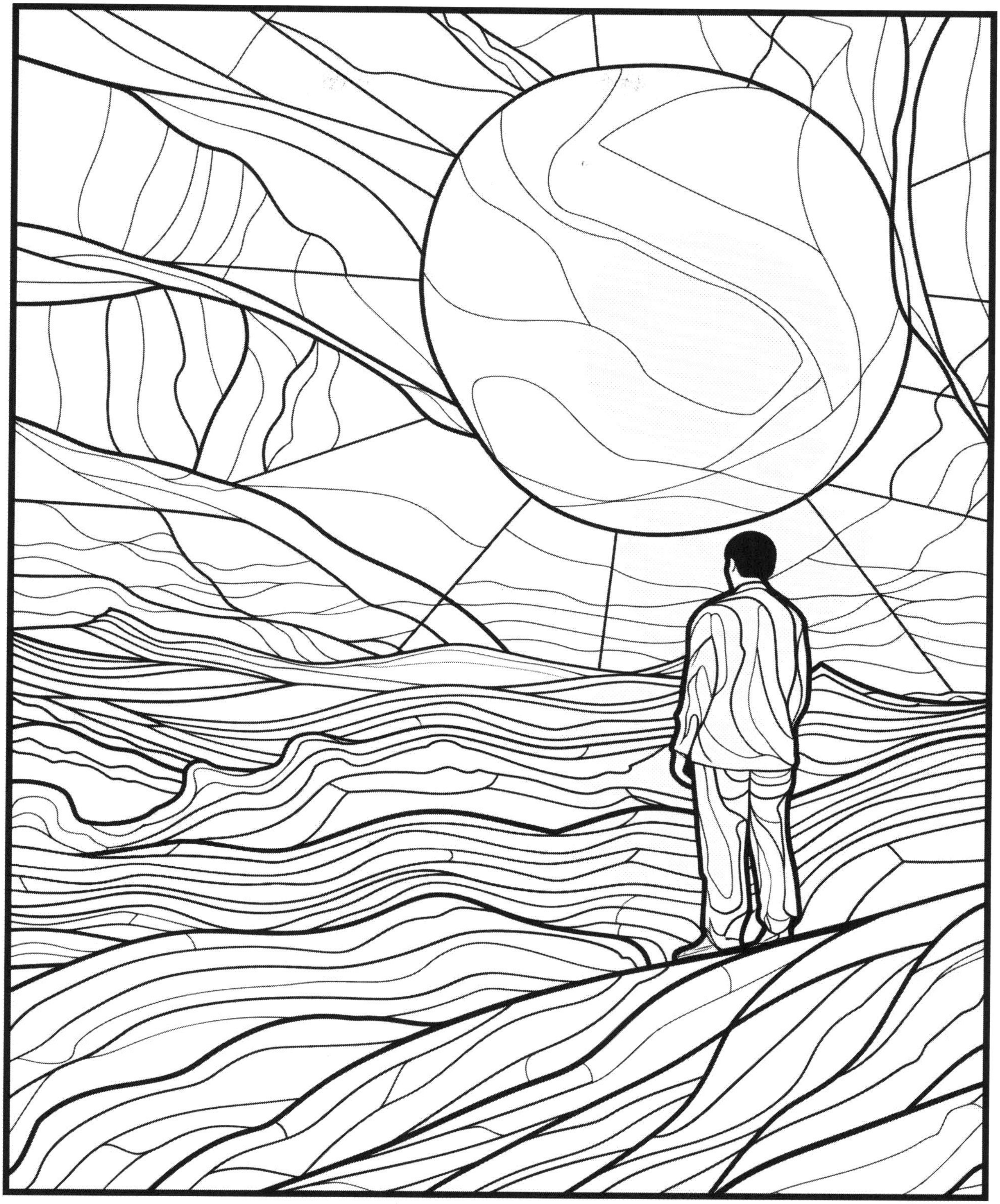

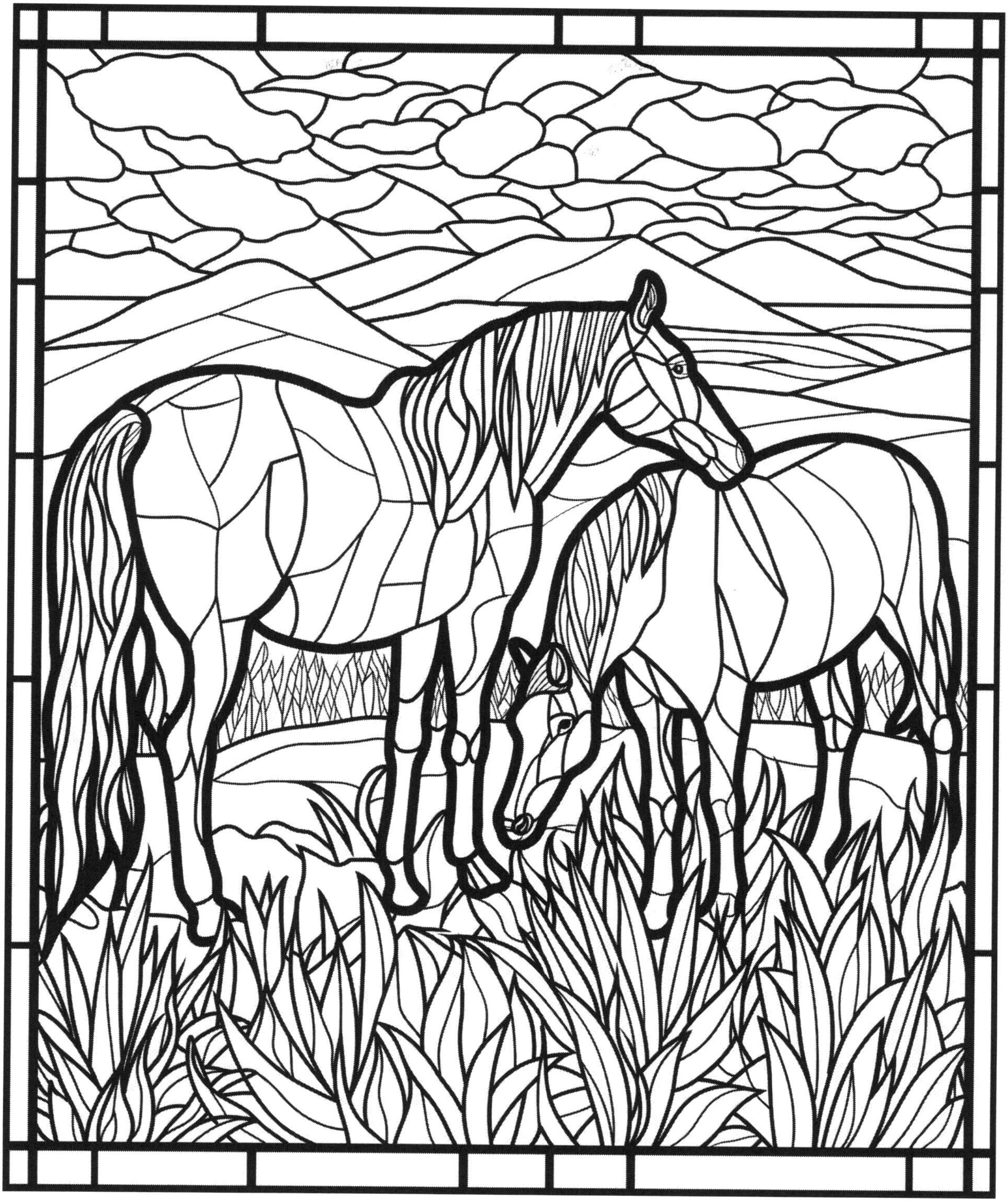

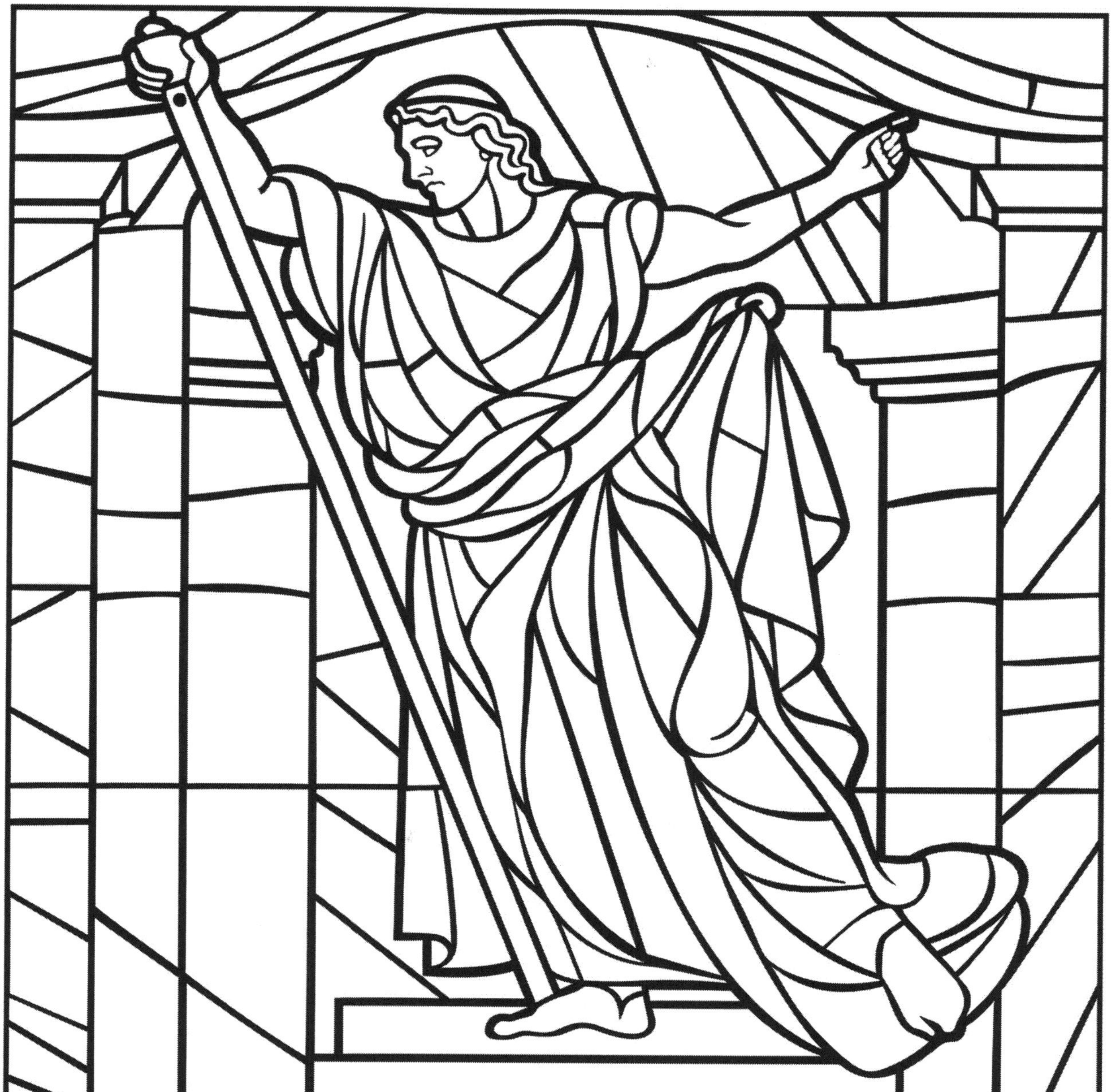

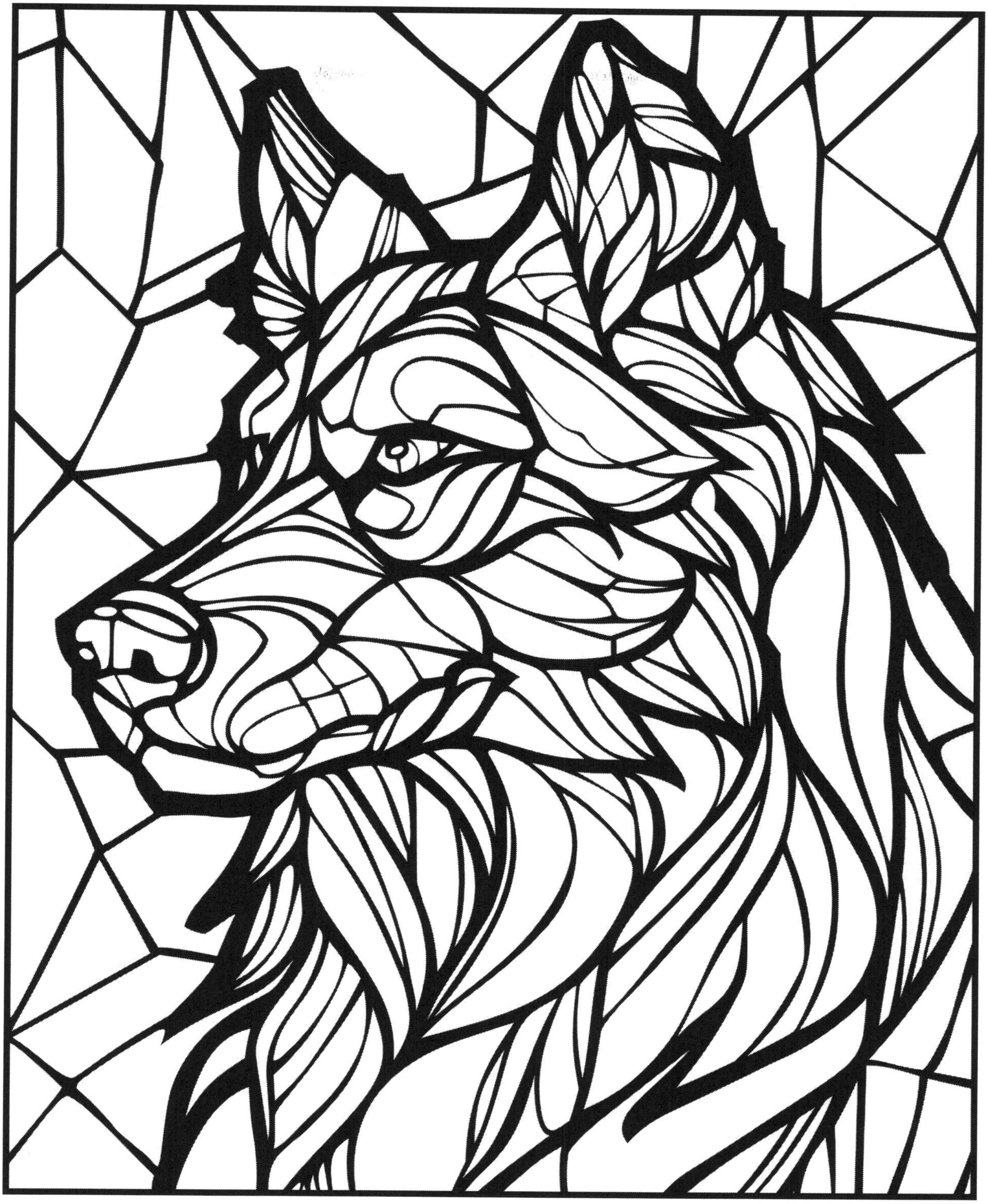

Made in the USA
Columbia, SC
08 October 2024